Finding Roger

An Improbably Theatrical Love Story

Rick Elice

KINGSWELL

Los Angeles • New York

To the theater,
and all the people
who live there. . . .

CONTENTS

A Sabbath Speech
Annual LGBTQ Service / JUNE 5, 2015
Congregation Rodeph Sholom—New York City

Someone in a big hurry asked Hillel, the great rabbi
and scholar, to summarize the meaning of the entire Old
Testament, while standing on one foot.

Hillel's reply: "What is hateful to you, do not do to your
neighbor. That's the whole thing; the rest is the explanation of
this. Now go and study it!"

Following in the hallowed tradition of Hillel, Roger Rees—
my partner of thirty-three years and my husband for four—has
his own standing-on-one-foot philosophy of life, concise
enough to fit on a T-shirt, and true enough to come in all sizes:
BE JOLLY AND KIND; THAT'S ALL THAT MATTERS. Simple, short,
and sweetly true. A way to make the world a better place.

In the Jewish tradition, this is called *tikkun olam*—literally
to repair the world. But Roger was raised Church of England.
He only converted to Judaism twenty-five years ago. How
could he understand tikkun olam better than I do?

It turns out, of course, that Roger understands *everything*
better than I do. Which is why our decades together are such a
blessing for me.

And if tikkun olam is making the world a better place,
Roger teaches me every day that you make the world a better
place by first being a better man. Which for me was to be a
man worthy of him, of irreplaceable Rog—the person I knew,
from the moment I saw him, was my destiny. In fact, our being
together struck us both as "meant to be." *B'shert*, as they say.
This little story will explain why. It's a story that dates back to
our first meeting.

Actually, a couple of years before our first meeting.

It was 1979, and I was a young actor fresh out of Yale
Drama School. On the same day that I received my master's

degree, I wrote a letter to Trevor Nunn, then the artistic director of the Royal Shakespeare Company, saying, "Hey, I'm a brand-new Yale Drama MFA, and I'm getting on a plane and coming over to be in the RSC! Just tell me when to show up!" Two weeks later, I got a letter back from Nunn: "Sorry, we don't hire Americans."

Well, I was shattered. I mean, I had an MFA from Yale! And here's this SOB telling me that my MFA was DOA at the RSC.

Instead, I spent a couple of years at the American Repertory Theatre in Cambridge, Massachusetts. Then I came home to New York. It was 1981, the same year that the mammoth eight-and-a-half-hour production of *The Life and Adventures of Nicholas Nickleby*—directed by John Caird and that same Trevor Nunn—came to New York. Came? It *conquered*.

I was incensed: A year before *Nickleby*, *Amadeus*, another British play, came to Broadway with its fancy British actors and their fancy British accents—and hogged all the attention and all the awards. A year before that, *Piaf* did exactly the same thing, and regretted nothing.

Now *Nicholas Nickleby* shows up—and tickets are *a hundred bucks a pop!!* This was when Broadway tickets were only twenty dollars, you understand. And a hundred dollars to a twenty-five-year-old actor . . . well, it might as well have been a billion.

So here come the Brits, and the star of the show is on the cover of *Time* magazine, and the Royal Shakespeare Company is once again sucking up all the oxygen in New York, and I'm working a pathetic gig as an assistant stage manager in a truly awful musical in the basement of St. Peter's Church in the Citicorp building, and *I have had enough!*

So I go to Actors' Equity and I say, "I would like to start a committee to keep British actors out of Broadway." (British Out of Broadway—BOOB—that was our moniker.)

And literally, while I'm protesting the RSC's presence on Broadway, my dear friend Kate, a wonderful actress, calls me and says, "Rick, you have to go see *Nicholas Nickleby*. It'll change your life."

And I said, "I wouldn't go to that play with their hundred-dollar tickets if it was the last show on earth."

And Kate said, "But it's everything you love. It's brilliant. It will change your life." And I said, "I don't have a hundred dollars. And if I did, I sure wouldn't spend it on tickets. I'd spend it on food."

But the seed was sown. So I ask my father for a hundred bucks to buy food, and I go to the Plymouth Theatre on Forty-Fifth Street to buy a ticket to *Nicholas Nickleby* instead.

It's for Saturday, December 5, 1981. I'm sitting in the back on the side, with this giant Yale Drama School chip on my shoulder.

The actors are all milling about in the audience before the show starts. And all the way down front, kneeling at the edge of the stage, I see the most devastatingly beautiful person I've ever laid eyes on. *I wonder who* that *is*, I thought.

Turns out it was the guy playing Nicholas Nickleby.

By the time the play's over, more than eight hours later, I've learned a million times over that my friend Kate was quite correct. Being in the theater that day has profoundly changed my life.

At midnight, I stagger home to my little room on Fifty-Seventh Street. Flip on the TV to a new cable station that, like PBS, aired lots of British programs. A man in a tuxedo addresses the camera: "And now, the Royal Shakespeare Company production of Chekhov's *Three Sisters*." Turns out it features all the same actors I've just watched on Broadway. Including Roger. Then, at three in the morning, the man in the tuxedo approaches the camera again: "And now, the Royal Shakespeare Company production of Shakespeare's *Macbeth*." All the same actors again! Including Roger!

By the time the sun is coming up on Sunday morning, I've spent a whole day and night with the RSC. I've forgotten all about BOOB. All I can think of is Roger Rees. I feel compelled to write him a mash note.

I grab a yellow legal pad, and write a letter inviting Roger to come see me do a tap number at a benefit that very night for

New York Stage and Film company at the Milford Plaza Hotel. Just down the street from his theater. *What could be simpler?* I think. *Of course he'll come.*

I drop my letter off at his theater on the way to my hotel ballroom. I do my little tap dance. I help raise a little money. But—*unbelievably*—Roger doesn't show up. And a few weeks later, just after New Year's in 1982, the entire Royal Shakespeare Company decamps for England.

And that, I thought, was that.

Nevertheless, I'm obsessed. I turn my sad one-room apartment into a poor man's shrine to Roger. I find photos, interviews in magazines, ads in old newspapers. It's infatuation at DEFCON 5. It isn't sane or pretty. But it's the real thing.

Fast-forward ten months to September of 1982: I'm working part-time at an ad agency as a copywriter—a skill it turns out I had a knack for, which saved me from waiting tables.

There I am, writing ad copy for a new British musical that's coming to Broadway called *Cats*, directed, yet again, by my old nemesis and new-minted hero Trevor Nunn.

And because I'm working on the show, I get invited to the dress rehearsal on Wednesday, September 22, 1982. I'm sitting at the Winter Garden Theatre waiting for this *Cats* thing to begin, and walking down the aisle comes Roger Rees.

He was in New York for one day, between finishing shooting a new Bob Fosse film in Los Angeles, called *Star 80*, and starting rehearsals for a new Tom Stoppard play in London, called *The Real Thing*. He figured he'd swing by the theater to say hi to his pal, Trevor. I watch him down front, chatting and hugging and laughing. I begin to assemble a mental list of things to say to him when this *Cats* show is over.

Two hours later, it is. Roger is chatting, hugging, and laughing again. I go outside and wait at the stage door to introduce myself to him when he exits. Eventually he comes out onto Seventh Avenue, and I pounce.

I have all my questions prepared, about his performance in *Nickleby*, his performance in *Three Sisters*, his performance in *Macbeth*. I'm so happy! All I can think is, *I can't believe I'm talking to the man I've built a shrine to!*

Roger seems engaged; I guess actors enjoy talking about themselves. I steel myself for my final question: "Could we have dinner?"

He politely explains he's only in town for one day, and says no. I ask him again. A second time, he says no. I mull this for a moment.

Then I take a deep breath and say, "I'm not exactly sure why, but I feel if I don't ask you one more time, I'll regret it for the rest of my life. Are you sure you won't have dinner with me? I'm really not a stalker."

He smiles and says, "You might be just a teensy bit of a stalker. But alright."

The next day, September 23, I leave the office early to dismantle the shrine, and prepare *pigeon en croûte* in my sad little kitchen. It was inedible, but Roger was perfection.

We talked and talked until four in the morning, made out a bit, sang a few songs to each other, and then it was time for Roger to get in a car to go to the airport. Rog says, "Maybe you'll come over in six weeks and see *The Real Thing*. Here's my phone number in London."

"I don't know what it costs to call London, but I'm sure it's more than I can afford," I say.

He says, "Here's my address. Write. Write a lot. Write me lots of letters. I'll write back."

That same day, I was offered three jobs: a season at the Guthrie Theater in Minneapolis; an understudy gig for a new cabaret on Forty-Fourth Street; and a full-time copywriter position at the ad agency I've been working at part-time for a month.

I took the writing job, because I figured Minneapolis was even farther away from London than New York. And an acting job meant having only one day off a week. At the ad agency, I'd have whole entire weekends off. Which meant I could go to London for two whole entire days. And I'd have a steady paycheck to pay for the trips.

And I'd be writing; and Roger had told me to write. Over the next six weeks, I followed Roger's direction. I wrote and wrote. Copious letters, typed and in longhand. I wrote about my hopes, my fears, my opinions, my passions—pages and pages—surrendering to that great feeling when you don't want to hold anything back. You know, *intimacy*. And amazingly, astonishingly, *intimately*—Roger wrote back.

The Friday before Thanksgiving, I boarded a plane to London. The next morning, I was standing in Heathrow Airport at the crack of dawn, waiting for Roger. He'd promised to meet my plane. I was suddenly terrified: what if he didn't remember what I looked like?

I mean, I knew what *he* looked like, of course. He'd been on the cover of *Time* magazine. But what if he walked right past me and I was left standing at the gate—and suddenly, there he was! Right in front of me, sporting a thick black beard for his part in the play—which had opened the week before and was a smash hit for Stoppard and his stars, Felicity Kendal and Roger Rees. Somehow, even after six weeks of rehearsal and opening a play and being at the center of another whirlwind of attention on the other side of the world, Roger still remembered who I was. Golly.

We hop into his car, and he drives me through London to his house, south of the river Thames. The house is next door to his mother's house. And, it being Saturday, Roger has a matinee. So he introduces me to his mum, hands me a ticket to his show that night, tells me which tube train to take to the West End, and leaves.

The play, thank goodness, is wonderful. And Roger is wonderful in it. I spend the next ten days falling and falling and falling. Rog is by now introducing me as "my chap." I don't want to return to New York, but I board the plane with a goofy smile, because I am deeply, profoundly, *molecularly* in love.

I write more letters to Roger, and he writes back. It becomes a thing for us, letter-writing. A way to bridge the three thousand miles that separate us.

The other bridge was British Airways. I'm so besotted, I'm showing up at the British Airways ticket office every Friday for a standby ticket to London, arrive on Saturday, come back Sunday night.

A couple of months of these standby weekends, and bushels of letters later, the woman at British Airways asks me why I take so many trips, and I tell her I'm in love. "Do you believe in love?" I ask her.

She smiles and tells me to leave my passport at my office, and, for a year, she calls me every Friday morning to let me know whether it's a good weekend for standby. Sometimes she even upgrades me, "because," she says, "I too believe in love."

Three years later, three years of long-distance love and letter-writing, and flying to London, Germany, Switzerland, Los Angeles—wherever he was working—Roger and I, firmly a couple and besotted with each other, are at his house in London, painting the front room. Ecstatic domesticity.

He's got a file cabinet against one wall. Best way to move a file cabinet—first you take out all the drawers, then you move

the metal shell away from the wall, paint the wall, move the metal shell back, and replace the drawers.

I'm putting the top drawer back into the cabinet, and I notice a tab on top of the file in front. It says: RICK'S CORRESPONDENCE.

And I say, "*Awww* that's so sweet. You saved my letters."

I was so flattered. I mean, I saved everything from Roger, even the hairs from his comb.

I was obsessed, this I knew. But it never occurred to me that he would save anything from *me*.

Roger smiles. He says, "You wanna really freak out?" And he comes over to the file drawer, leafs through to the very front of it, and pulls out a folded piece of yellow legal paper. "I don't know why I saved this," he says, "but I did." It was the letter I'd written him a year before we met.

That's the moment I learned that, while I was standing outside of *Cats* thinking *I can't believe I'm talking to the man I've built a shrine to!* Roger was standing there thinking *I can't believe I'm talking to the guy who wrote me that letter.* Thirty-three years ago. Like I said, meant to be.

For thirty-three years, my knowing this wonderful person has made me a better man. Which makes it only fair that I work and write every day—letters, radio, and TV commercials, movie trailers, birthday cards, even a few Broadway shows— but I write and write and write. Because if you can get the right words in the right order you can nudge the world a little. You can make the world a better place.

That's what Roger's made me want to do from that first September 23, when he said, "Write." Try to make the world a better place. *Tikkun olam.*

Thank you, Roger. Shabbat shalom.

THERE IS NO CURE

HELLO, DEAR FRIENDS AND FAMILY—

This is a tough one to write. Our beautiful and brilliant friend
Roger has what's called glioblastoma, which is a very shitty brain
cancer. He's been struggling with it since October, when on a beautiful
fall day, he started walking into people and things—and our lives
changed forever. There is no cure.

I won't go here into the details of his fight for the past nine months.
In brief, there have been two major surgeries, two rounds of radiation,
lots of chemo, lots of visits to doctors and hospitals, lots of fear, and lots
of love. Somehow—and his team at the hospital said it was "beyond
remarkable"—Roger managed, in the midst of this hell, to rehearse and
perform a Broadway musical, *The Visit*. That's not a typo; you read
that right. On March 4, the man had brain surgery. On March 10, he
was back in rehearsal. On March 26, he started previews on Broadway.
I mean, what a guy! And he had the most wonderful time, which made
it especially heartbreaking when, after it became too difficult for him to
speak, he had to take leave of the show in May.

Here we are, five weeks later. Roger's just returned home from
sixteen days in the hospital defeating aspirated pneumonia. (He's still
a strong, fit man, except for the brain cancer.) We talked about what
to do next, and he said, "Just take me home." So that's where we are
now. We organized twenty-four-hour nursing care, and Roger's in good
spirits. It'll take a bit of getting used to, being fussed over and having
strangers in the house—but soon, they won't be strangers.

Meanwhile, people have been checking in from all over the world,
and we're both overwhelmed by how much everyone loves Roger. Not
that we didn't know it, and appreciate it all these years. But the rush of
it is magnificent, and the volume of it, exhilarating. To the extent that
it's also a bit exhausting for Rog, give me a holler if you want to drop
by. We'd love to see you, but sometimes the boy needs a rest, or just a
good sit in the sun. There'll be lots of that.

9

ROGER HEADS HOME

Here are some photos of the hospital stay just ended.

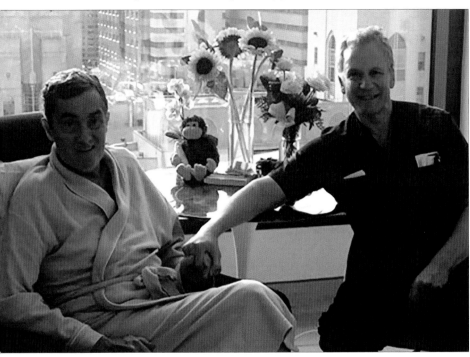

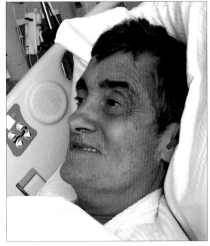

Look at this gorgeous face on Sunday, June 28, 2015, in the hospital.

We left beautiful flowers for our beautiful nurses . . .

. . . and came home to the first nasturtium of the season! Almost like it was planned.

By the end of the afternoon, Roger was giving instructions to the gardener . . .

Saturday, July 4: *Roger and our great-niece, Vivienne, painted the town. Her parents (Jeremy and Nicole) flew her to New York to say hi to Uncle Rog.*

Sunday, July 5: *Two hours in New York's Central Park, with Roger's nurse, Prince Darkwa, including visits to the Great Lawn and Shakespeare Garden.*

Tomorrow, a new week. How great to be home!

Lots of love,
Rick and Rog

A BIT OF CONTEXT

I'M A BIG ONE FOR CONTEXT. So I thought I'd give you a bit of mine. There's so much of our life together that we keep private, Roger and I: the knowing and being known, the mask slipped from the face, those parts of ourselves that belong just to each other in all their nonverbal, inexpressible glory. But, as Roger's has been a public life as well, we thought we'd celebrate some of that life, and our life together. No time like the present.

I first got to know him, really got to know him, when Rog was rehearsing and then playing in the original production of Tom Stoppard's *The Real Thing*, which opened at the Strand Theatre (now the Novello) in London's West End in November 1982. ("The mask slipped from the face"—a quote from Tom's play—started this free-associating, consciousness-streaming . . . so bear with me.)

The play starred Felicity Kendal ("Flick") as Annie and Roger Rees as Henry, very possibly one of greatest roles written for an actor in the twentieth century. (Humbly submitted.) It was directed by Tom's frequent collaborator at the time, Peter Wood. When I first saw it, about a week after it opened, on the first of a lifetime of trips to London, the play was so sexy, and Flick and Roger were so cracklingly good together, that my knees ached.

Here's a photo from that world premiere production, the very first time *The Real Thing* took life onstage: you can see why I never stood a chance.

> "I don't think writers are sacred, but words are. They deserve respect. If you get the right ones in the right order, you can nudge the world a little. . . ."

Bless you, Tom Stoppard.

The original cast of *Real Thing* stayed with the play for about a year, at the end of which Roger canceled our planned trip to Greece in favor of . . . wait for it . . . making a film with some fellow named Laurence Olivier. It has always been futile to argue over canceled trips and vacations with Rog; what could possibly be your premise? ("I don't care if you get to make a movie with the greatest actor in the world! I bought all this sunscreen!" Doesn't hold water, does it?)

At any rate, the night before he winged his way to Limoges to lens with Larry, Roger asked me to shave off his *Real Thing* beard. This was not in my skill set. A couple of hours later, and no doubt sorry he'd asked, Rog packed for France. He left the next morning, bloodied but clean-shaven.

Fast-forward to last Friday, when it was time for Rog to get smooth enough to kiss our great-niece Vivi on Saturday. I shaved Roger again, on the terrace—so I didn't have to worry about being neat, neatness being another of the many skills *not* in my skill set.

Here, in celebration of the minutiae that comes to represent our lives as much as any of the gargantuae, is the before-and-after of our ablutive adventure.

Before shave, in silent contemplation of blood to be spilled . . .

And, a half hour later, smoothish in time for our beautiful niece-ette. Notice the raw red neck of my victim. Rest assured that buckets of Kiehl's were applied to stanch the stinging.

More as it occurs. Thanks to everyone who replied to the first Roger Report. I cried and I cried, and now that my darling is stirring in his cot, I will read each of your comments to him, and we'll figure out what, for today at least, is what.

Lots of love,
Rick and Rog

ON THIS DAY

I CAME ACROSS THIS PHOTO taken exactly six years ago, the day Roger became an American citizen. It was a long time coming, and he was very excited, even though he had to take a test. Rog is very weak on American history. He could never grasp the concept of a bicameral legislative body. He could not remember the three branches of government. He could not—even after playing John Adams in *1776* (Peter Stone, the late, much-lauded screenwriter and librettist, loved him as Adams)—list the thirteen original colonies. I mean, this is a man who refers to the American Revolution as "The Skirmish." I figured he didn't stand a chance.

Fortunately for Rog, his interviewer recognized him from *The West Wing*. He asked Roger who his favorite actor is. Roger said, "Harvey Keitel." (News to me.) The fellow said, "Really? I love Harvey Keitel. Do you know him?" Roger said, "Very well." (News to me.) The interviewer said, "That is just so cool. Is he nice?" Roger said, "Nicest man in the world."

The interviewer, thus reassured, stamped Roger's application, and his American citizenship was in the bag. Thank you, Harvey Keitel.

After the ceremony downtown, we had a red-white-and-blue breakfast at Bubby's in lower Manhattan. Strawberry and blueberry pancakes with whipped cream. And my British bloke was suddenly my Yankee doodle. Six years ago today.

Five years ago today, Roger and Ian McKellen, his buddy from the RSC days, having taken London by storm, were barnstorming the rest of the world in *Waiting for Godot* (photo above). That included every major city in Australia and New Zealand.

And, unforgettably for Rog, a stint in South Africa, including a performance of the play in front of an audience that had never seen a play or been in a theater. This was in Khayelitsha Township. They performed the play on a bare rostrum in a gymnasium with holes in the roof and birds flying in and out. Daylight was the lighting. Roger said it was his favorite performance of the play, and the audience understood it and delighted in it as no audience in London or Sydney or Melbourne or Adelaide or Brisbane or Darwin or Auckland or Wellington or Christchurch ever had. When the production came to New York two years ago, Ian played it with Pat Stewart.

When Roger returned from *Godot*, our friend, the Broadway producer Stuart Oken, suggested he replace Nathan Lane in *The Addams Family*. Roger played opposite Bebe Neuwirth, his longtime pal from his *Cheers* days; they'd done a bunch of plays together over the years, including an unforgettable *Taming of the Shrew*, directed by Rog, at Williamstown Theatre Festival in 1999.

Bebe Neuwirth and Rog in The Addams Family *(Broadway, 2011)*

Three months into Roger's run, Bebe was replaced by Brooke Shields, who, it turns out, has legs as gorgeous as every other part of her, inside and out. Rog had such a wonderful time with all the talented people in that cast; he was in a perpetually good mood. So much so that he came home from the show on the night after the New York State Senate voted to allow same-sex marriage, got down on his knee, and proposed. And then he even asked me to marry him. (*Rimshot!*) That was four years ago last week. We were very happy the other day, June 26, when the Supreme Court made it legal coast to coast.

Brooke Shields with Rog in
The Addams Family *(Broadway, 2011)*

Three years ago today, we celebrated the one-hundredth performance of *Peter and the Starcatcher* on Broadway. Our dear pal, Christian Borle, had just left the show, a Tony in tow, to resume his television commitments; but the show played on and on. The photo here was taken on opening night, and while Adam Chanler-Berat, Celia Keenan-Bolger, and Christian were the stars of the evening, the stars of the experience were Roger and Alex Timbers, who made something very special for all of us involved. Something I'm thankful for every day of my life.

Left to right: Rog, Christian Borle, Alex Timbers, and me on opening night

Roger and Alex were a formidable directing team. They are wildly different people, from wildly different backgrounds and entirely different generations. And yet, they worked together so seamlessly, you could never have guessed there were two minds at play. I'm just the lucky guy who got asked into the sandbox.

Two years ago today, Roger was heading off to Denver to launch the first national tour of *Peter* at the city's Center for the Performing Arts (see photo to the right). The show that started in the back of a log cabin in Williamstown was suddenly taking up residence in an opera house.

Roger was there every step of the way, even though he was increasingly weighed down with a whole different *Stache*—the one he was growing for Terence Rattigan's *The Winslow Boy* (see photo below), which began rehearsals back in New York immediately after *Peter* was up and running in Denver.

What a great production *Winslow*, directed by Lindsay Posner, was. It played a block away from a revival of another play written in the same year, *The Glass Menagerie*, with the sublime Celia K-B. Also in town at the same time was *Waiting for Godot*, with Pat Stewart, who had replaced Rog opposite Ian McKellen.

"The Sirs" could often be found hanging out backstage at Roundabout with Rog, comparing facial hair no doubt.

Which brings us to a year ago.

Roger in his acclaimed turn as Arthur Winslow in The Winslow Boy *(Broadway, 2013)*

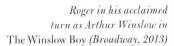

One brief year. The summer before everything turned upside down.

We had just returned from The Old Globe in San Diego, where Roger had directed (brilliantly, hilariously—and in the freakin' ROUND!!) a new musical called *Dog and Pony* (music and lyrics by Michael Patrick Walker).

The cast of Dog and Pony. *Front row (left to right): Jon Patrick Walker, Eric Morris, Michael Patrick Walker; back row (left to right): me, Beth Leavel, Barry Edelstein, (artistic director of The Globe), Nicole Parker, Roger, and Heidi Blickenstaff*

Which brings us to today: the day (give or take) that the original cast recording of *The Visit* hits the stores. I was being a Tony nominator on April 27 when the cast and orchestra of *The Visit* were making this record. Just scant weeks ago, but for me the sound of Roger's voice—today just a gentle wisp of a whisper—so recently so robust is such a gift. So, apologies, friends, for this sentimental trip down six years of memory lanes. These are only the barest scratch on the surface of the rich life Roger has led every day—as you know. And six years only because of the flag shot, which I came across today looking for something else. We don't have a life in pictures, we don't commemorate every envelope opened, every adjective offered. We have

Roger and Dolores Conchita Figueroa del Rivero Montestuco Florentino
Carnemacarel del Fluente (aka Chita Rivera). Look at 'em.
Don't you just want to be a member of this club?
The Visit—*Williamstown, 2014*

our work, we have what we learn from our work to apply to our next
work. And we have our family and friends.

Love to all of you from both of us. Now Roger will check out the
Wimbledon matches. He grew up not far from the stadium, and this
has always been a big week for him (even though he's now an American
citizen).

X
Rick and Rog

THE IMPORTANT PEOPLE TO ROGER REES

I THINK I'VE GOTTEN A LITTLE CARRIED AWAY HERE, but it's been a tough morning and there's some things I need to say and some people I need to point out.

First, a look at Roger Rees. Just because.

Let's just consider that beautiful face for a moment before reading on.

Now—"The Important People to Roger Rees": because I don't have endless supplies of digital photos, I'm selecting snaps to represent whole swaths of the human population. So please bear with me, and allow me, a cipher in this great account, to work on your imaginations. . . .

Think when I talk of actors or writers, directors or producers, that you see them strutting in their paths upon the stage. And when you meet a family, that you have spent a lifetime of weekends and holidays with them before now. For 'tis your thoughts that here must help my hands, cramming the accomplishments of many years into this humble "Report."

So may you gently read and kindly judge this entry. And so, in no particular order: the photo (left) is of Alex Timbers and Roger, directors of *Peter and the Starcatcher* (offering notes to the playwright, no doubt). Alex's body of work will be studied, analyzed, and copied for the next hundred years, and we're in awe of him. But this photo represents all the directors who helped to make Roger—among them Trevor Nunn, John Caird, John Barton, Richard Cottrell, Peter Wood, Adrian Noble, Peter Hall, John Doyle, Sean Mathias, Greg Doran, Ron Daniels, Joe Mantello, Jerry Zaks, Mike Nichols, Nicky Martin, Mark Lamos, Barry Edelstein, Brian Kulick, Lindsay Posner, Michael Hoffman, Ric Burns, Stanley Donen, Julie Taymor, Bob Fosse, and Mel Brooks. And all the dozens of great directors whose names I'm forgetting because this is so hard to write. But thank you, all of you. For Roger.

And for all the British actors who've inspired Rog, and made him laugh, cry, grow—sometimes all at once. Beginning with his dearest Judi Dench and Ian McKellen, there's Nick Grace, Barbara Leigh-Hunt, Richard Pasco, Donald Sinden, Alan Howard, Ken Branagh, Edward Petherbridge, Emily Richard, Suzanne Bertish, Frances Barber, Felicity Kendal, Polly Adams, Francesca Annis, Harriet Walter, Jane Lapotaire, Jane Carr, Ralph

Ian McKellen and Judi Dench in Trevor Nunn's legendary Macbeth, *1976. Roger played Malcolm.*

Reader, Douglas Gordon, Nigel Hawthorne, Helen Mirren, Virginia McKenna, Sara Kestelman, Lisa Harrow, Eileen Atkins, Jude Law, Peggy Ashcroft, Alan Bates, Laurence Olivier, and Roger's private hero, Ralph Richardson. And on and on and on, if only I could think of them all. . . .

Celia Keenan-Bolger, Rog, and Christian Borle / April 15, 2012

And his American actor friends and inspirations: Adam Chanler-Berat, Celia Keenan-Bolger, Christian Borle (pictured above left to right); Dana Ivey; Kathleen Turner; Meryl Streep; Cynthia Nixon; Cherry Jones; Brooke Shields; Jennifer Van Dyck; Matt Letscher; Didi Lovejoy; Sharon Lawrence; Katie Finneran; Tom Bloom; Jean Smart; John Benjamin Hickey; Nancy Marchand; Kyle Fabel; Joel Grey; Brian Murray; John Conlee; Heidi Blickenstaff; Beth Leavel; Nicole Parker; Eric Morris; Jon Patrick Walker; Catherine Brunell; Kate Burton; Victor Garber; Greg Hildreth, Arnie Burton, Teddy Bergman, Matt D'Amico, Kevin Del Aguila, Rick Holmes, Karl Kenzler, Dave Rossmer, Steve Rosen, Carson Elrod, Isaiah Johnson, Brandon Dirden, Sammy Wright, Jason Ralph, Betsy Hogg, Megan Stern, Joey deBettencourt, Nicole Lowrance, John Sanders, Carl Howell, Ben Schrader, and *all* the Starcatchers; Alessandro Nivola, Mary Elizabeth Mastrantonio, and all the Winslows; Harvey Fierstein; Marin Mazzie; Jason Danieley, Mary Beth Peil, David Garrison, Chita Rivera, and all *The Visit* crowd; Carrie Preston; Jim Stanek; David Aaron Baker; Michael Emerson; Nick Wyman; Uma Thurman; Martin Sheen, John Spencer, Allison Janney, Stockard Channing, Richard Schiff, and the *West Wing*-ers; Ted Danson, Kirstie Alley, Woody Harrelson, Kelsey Grammer, John Ratzenberger, Rhea Perlman, George Wendt, and everybody at *Cheers*. And, of course, Bebe, who bonded with Roger at a table read for *Cheers* in 1989, and always loved being onstage with him.

Roger, with Bebe Neuwirth, in Williamstown's Taming of the Shrew *in 1999—I swear, the sexiest production of that play in the history of the whole world ever.*

Apologies again and again to everyone I've omitted. I'm writing this while sitting with our wonderful cantor, Rebecca Garfein, as she sings Roger's favorite High Holiday song (*L'dor V'ador*); our esteemed rabbi, Robert Levine; and Tom Kirdahy, Roger's producer on *The Visit*, who came by at the same time. They're now having an extraordinary conversation, and Rog and I are listening and learning. Anyhow, focus is a bit split, so forgive me my sins of omission.

That's Tom Schumacher (at right), producing a Christmas morning divertissement with no less élan than he produced *Aladdin*.

I don't know where I'd be without Tom, but this isn't about me. One of his greatest attributes is his appreciation of talent. And his appreciation of Roger always makes me want to hug him. Please let Tom signify all the producers who've believed in Roger's talents, and kept him working constantly for fifty years. It's a very long list, but these names pop up instantly: Tom Kirdahy, Todd Haimes, Scott Rudin, André Bishop, Peter Schneider, John Wells, James Burrows, Max Mutchnick, Ric Burns, Nancy Gibbs, Nina Essman, Marcia Goldberg, Greg Schaffert, Tom Smedes, Catherine Schreiber, Eva Price, Lynne Meadow, Barry Edelstein, Roger Berlind, Daryl Roth, Jordan Roth, Michael Ritchie, Jenny Gersten, Mandy Greenfield, Manny Azenberg, Michael Codron, Liz McCann, Nelle Nugent, Jimmy Nederlander, Phil Smith, Bernie Jacobs, and Jerry Schoenfeld. Bravo!

Roger (pencil in mouth), Peter Wood (facing camera), Felicity Kendal (back to camera), and Tom Stoppard (in profile) rehearsing the world premiere production of The Real Thing

Let Sir Tom Stoppard represent all the writers who have given words to Roger and given Roger his voice. From Shakespeare and Shaw to Ahrens and Flaherty. From Terence Rattigan and Terry Johnson to Peter Stone and Robbie Baitz. And from Jimmy Burrows and Aaron Sorkin to Terrence McNally and Kander & Ebb: *write on!*

With enough time, Roger would create a show about how much each of you mean to him; companion pieces to his *What You Will* tribute—so good, and so richly, warmly, sweetly Roger—to Mr. Shakespeare.

And now, friends. Yes, let me now move on to friends. All of you reading this, for example—and hundreds more that I don't have a way to reach or the brain cells to remember right now—who have been stand-up people, and stood up for Rog.

Jessica Brickman and Sophie Brickman Eisenberg, representing their parents, Marshall and Nina Brickman: the four of them met Roger and me decades ago. They are individually and collectively finer, funnier, brighter, more moral, and more loyal than the rest of the planet. Let them stand in for all of Roger's fine and funny and constantly generous friends. All of you that Roger wants in his lifeboat. All of you who want Roger in yours. Cheers!

This is me with Jessica Brickman (left) and Sophie Brickman Eisenberg (right), at Sophie's wedding.

Nancy Coyne—who's known me as long as Roger. In fact, exactly as long. She's been our gyroscope all these years, pointing us in the right direction, even if it meant pointing us away from her. Let Nancy stand in for all of Roger's friends who've guided him and delivered him, on time and in excellent condition. Such a list of Roger's friends would

*Me and Nancy Coyne,
my best friend since 1982*

be hundreds of names long, but if
you're getting this report, this
means you! Thank you! Thank
you! Thank you!

Let Christian Borle stand in for
every one of you who ever thanked
Roger for the light that comes from

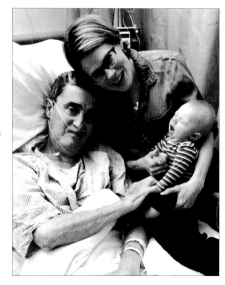

*Roger and
Christian
Borle*

him so effortlessly and in such
endless supply. Roger owes so
much to so many talented people.

And let William E. Conlee
(yawning, in the arms of his
mommy, Celia K-B, right) stand
in for all the children that Roger's
had over the years. Calm down,
Page Six fans: I mean, children as
art. Roger feels that every part he
plays, and every play he directs,
is his baby. And, after fifty years
onstage, this is one fecund proud
papa, our Mister Rees.

And finally, family.

Roger lost his dad when he was still a teenager. He lost his brother and his mum back in 1989. Except for his dear cousins, the Weedens (who spent a couple of days here in New York with us in February) his family has been my family. My parents, I'm proud to say, call Roger their son-in-law.

Rog and his mother-in-law, Roz Elice

Rog and his niece, Jennifer, and me

Rog is showing off his first-ever Valentine's Day card from his great-niece, Mollie.

Mollie with her dad, Eric Gatz

Roger with his nephew, Jeremy, and Dexter, in the blue tag and leash

Roger's fave gals: Nicole Elice, Vivienne Elice, Roz Elice, Mollie Gatz, Jennifer Gatz, and JoAnn Elice

Roger's father-in-law, Harold, surrounded by Mollie, Jen, and Roz

And, here's the closer: May 5, just eight weeks ago, Roger's birthday. With his brother-in-law, Mike, and his sister-in-law, JoAnn . . . and the lucky so-and-so on the far left: the husband.

God bless us, everyone—for knowing this wonderful guy. And God bless Roger for being known. We had to start him on a little bit of morphine today to help him breathe, and get more oxygen into his lungs. He's still alert and comfortable. But we want to keep him from getting pneumonia again.

That's our mission. May we be able to hold it at bay for a bit. Fingers crossed!!

We love you all the day.
Rog and Rick

Illustration of me and Rog
(The New Yorker *magazine, May 2012)*

CURTAIN CALL

LAST NIGHT, AFTER SOME HOURS of respiratory distress, Roger was relaxing comfortably in bed. Near him, an open window, through which he could hear me, my brother, my sister-in-law, my aunt, and our friends Beth Leavel, Marty Moran, Bob Martin, and Jorge Vargas. Roger was too weak to sit with us on the terrace, so we spoke loudly, laughed lustily, and gobbled the world's greatest Russian babka (courtesy of Sophie and Dave Eisenberg). It was a beautiful sunset and a cool evening, and we lingered outside Roger's window until about 7:30.

Then it was time for everyone to leave, and Roger and I were going to hunker down for another long night of shallow breathing and loose coughing. Challenging, but not impossible. And there was always Wimbledon to look forward to. We were going to watch on the big TV in the library.

At 7:45 we were all standing around Roger, who was propped up in bed like a lord, listening to me yammer on (me, yammer? Impossible!) about something or other—just trying to be amusing, you understand—and everyone was laughing; and Roger was rolling his eyes perhaps (although he did seem a bit exhausted), and all was right with the world.

At 7:55 everyone leaned in to kiss him good night, and I saw our friends out to the elevator, which came in due course and took our pals away.

I walked back into the apartment. My brother waved me into Roger's room. "His breathing's stopped," he said. I couldn't understand what he meant at first. Roger was right there, looking at me. And then I realized he wasn't breathing. Eight o'clock. He had an entrance to make—or in this case, the most graceful, utterly modest exit one could imagine. He said good night to his guests, and when they departed, so did he.

Not a groan or a cough or a syllable of complaint. Not a shudder or a moan. Just a beautiful, simple, profound exit. Pursued by my heart. My broken heart.

My brother said, "The damn tumor can't hurt him anymore. After nine months of torture, most of it in secret, Roger is better at last." And he is.

For all the decades I've known him, he's made me feel like the luckiest man in any room. Everyone loves Roger—and for good reasons, for many reasons, for *worlds* of excellent reasons. But I, for thirty-three years, have been the bloke who got to go home with him.

With this man, this remarkable, beautiful man.

Believe me, I know how lucky that makes me. And now, how unspeakably, indescribably sad. Now stops the noblest heart I've ever known. Good night, sweet prince. And flights of angels sing thee to thy rest.

We're going to organize a small funeral on Monday, and get back in touch about a proper memorial sometime after the summer. A lot of folks have things they'd like to say; things I'd love a theater full of people to hear. Stay tuned for those details. And until then, remember our gentle boy.

MICHAEL ELICE / Eulogy at Roger's Funeral, July 13, 2015

I met Roger thirty-two years ago. It was my thirtieth birthday and my wife, JoAnn, and I were in London to celebrate. Rick arranged for us to see his "buddy Roger" in *The Real Thing* in the West End and we were to go backstage and meet him in his dressing room. That was a new experience for us—meeting a star in his dressing room!

Actually, the man we met projected very little of a star persona, but was instead a sweet, friendly, handsome man in a very unglamorous room with a bare lightbulb hanging from the ceiling and a birthday cake glowing with thirty-one candles. The cake was held by Rick, who had flown to London to surprise me. An experience I have never forgotten.

Our relationship with Roger continued, mostly across the pond, as his relationship with Rick progressed through courting to falling in love to, ultimately, when it became legal to do so in New York, getting married. For thirty-three years, Roger's been my brother-in-law and uncle to my kids, and he had all of us, his family.

Roger turned out to be one of the funnier people I've met. He became known as "silly Uncle Rog"—the perfect complement to "crazy Uncle Rick." The boys would come out to our home and the homes of our friends, our extended family, for holiday dinners, bar and bat mitzvahs, proms, and many of our children's weddings. Birthdays and anniversaries were marked by original cards "made with love but often in haste." Roger, master of the English language, tried to teach us the basics of cockney English. He was able to write birthday books with as many words that rhymed with a name as he could think of, and set them to some ridiculous narrative.

Of note, my granddaughter Mollie, his great niece, took an immediate liking to Rog, yet was suspicious of Rick. This upset my brother no end. Mollie and Vivi, his other great niece, would howl when he would greet them with his usual "Hello, Darling!" He would say silly things, make funny faces, wear silly hats and disguises, and delight them.

As for JoAnn and me, we had another couple of friends with whom we loved to be. We have always enjoyed hanging out with Rick and Rog. They were both so amusing, yet we could discuss serious topics, current events, and enjoy a perspective that was different from others' points of view. Mind you, Roger had no qualms about telling us whom he thought was dreadful or stupid. Somehow, Rog could do that without ever sounding mean.

While he was a consummate professional for fifty years in the theater, his greatest role was that of husband, brother, and "guncle." We knew him as a kind, sensitive, thoughtful man who loved us, loved our parents, loved our children, our grandchildren, all of our dogs, and random old people. He was nonmaterialistic, but always shared his experiences. He would bring souvenirs from his travels: an autographed cocktail napkin from the White House, a T-shirt from Dublin, and lots of swag from opening night parties and charity events. None of these things mattered to Rog, so he would "regift" them for Hanukkah and birthdays.

Roger, you were "The Real Thing." As my dad always says whenever we part, "Never say good-bye, say so long." Today I would like to quote Roger. When he signed off a phone call or was leaving us, he never said good-bye either. He always said, "Lots of love and God bless."

Rog—from all of the family who loves you deeply: lots of love and God bless.

RICK ELICE / Eulogy at Roger's Funeral, July 13, 2015

I wasn't sure how to do this. I'm not, as most of you know, a pithy person. So it seemed like a possibly dangerous invitation when the funeral director said, "You can have the room as long as you like." How am I supposed to distill a life like Roger's into a couple of benign paragraphs, a few clever anecdotes? That's for a cocktail party, not for here. How am I supposed to tell the story of how we met—one of the great love stories, I think— when so many of you have already heard it? More than once. . . .

Borrowing money from my parents to see *Nicholas Nickleby*. Watching Roger in three plays in twenty-four hours, two of them on television, then rewinding and watching them again and again. The ignored (and later recovered) note inviting him to see me perform at a theater benefit. The introduction behind the Winter Garden Theatre. The first date, talking all night, until he had to catch a plane in the morning. The truckloads of letters, the phone calls, the "business trips" to London just to be close to him for one little day. The ferocious, burning desire to be with this man that made me chase him literally around the world. And how I'd do it all again in a second for one more day or one more night.

But I'm not gonna tell that story. I think if Roger has to sit through that story again, he'll rise right up and walk out of the room. And we can't very well have that.

We can, however, have some Shakespeare. Roger asked for this to be read; he read it twenty-six years ago when his brother, Andy, died at the age of forty-one. I was there, and it was exquisitely painful and beautiful as Roger spoke it. It's from act 4 of *Cymbeline*, but I won't describe the plot to you, because nobody's ever been able to describe the plot to *Cymbeline*. They are about to perform it in the park next week, so if you go—when you hear this, think of Roger. And try to hear Roger Rees speaking this now:

Fear no more the heat o' the sun;
Nor the furious winter's rages,
Thou thy worldly task hast done—
Home art gone, and taken thy wages;
Golden lads and girls all must,
As chimney sweepers come to dust.

Think and we will hear thee.
Nothing ill come near thee!
Quiet consummation have;
And renowned be thy grave!

But no one wants a funeral that is merely sad. Especially this one.

So here's some backstory about Roger you may not know, and which might work as a leavening agent.

Roger first became acquainted with William Shakespeare when he joined the Royal Shakespeare Company as a spear-carrier. He and his friend Ben Kingsley joined together. It was 1967.

The first production they were in was *The Taming of the Shrew*. They played silent, nonspeaking huntsmen. And they were good. They were so good, they went on to play silent, nonspeaking huntsmen in nearly every Shakespeare play. Both Ben and Roger eventually got to play Hamlet for the company, but those early days were spent learning their craft and carrying spears, shields, and Dame Peggy Ashcroft around the stage.

Ben, of course, went on to win an Oscar and to be knighted by the Queen of England. About seven years ago now, Roger could be seen playing a surgeon on *Grey's Anatomy*. In a three-episode arc.

I blame myself. Because Roger moved to America for me. But on behalf of the hundreds of friends in this room, aren't we glad he did?

My friend Nancy Coyne suggested that I make this eulogy the final Roger Report. The last in the series of updates I sent around over the past few days that most of you have gotten. That seemed like a great idea, until I realized I need to do one more Roger Report, with some information I'll try to send out later today or tomorrow.

Then my friend Tom Schumacher came by and said something to cheer me up—and it struck me as a great closing line. Now, opening lines are very important. They have to gather the audience close, make them put aside their workaday world, and start them listening. But closing lines must be definitive, provocative, memorable. Here's one, for example: *My extraordinary husband is gone.*

Look at that sentence. First of all, to be able to use the word *husband*, and not mean it euphemistically. To have lived long enough for that to be the case, when for twenty-nine of our thirty-three years together, there were many words for what Roger and I were to each other, but no one word that stood for all. Roger so loved it, when four years ago, we finally had a word for what we are. We high-fived two weeks ago when the Supreme Court decision was handed down. It was Friday, June 26—four years to the day that Roger proposed to me.

And then the phrase *extraordinary husband.* How incredibly blessed we are, Roger and I, to have found an extraordinary husband in each other.

How easy it would have been for us never to have met, never to have wooed, never to have won each other. How ordinary my life would otherwise have been without my extraordinary husband.

It's easy for me to tell you how extraordinary Roger is. Extraordinarily kind, extraordinarily talented, extraordinarily achieved . . . extraordinarily thoughtful, extraordinarily gentle, extraordinarily curious . . . extraordinarily patient, extraordinarily sentimental, extraordinarily affectionate.

This morning Trevor Nunn wrote me: "Roger was inspirational. I think of that iconic poster for *Nicholas Nickleby* and there he is, punching the air, and it's a thrilling image of determination, defiance, optimism, good fighting evil, and dauntless courage. Every one of those ingredients is in Nicholas, but every one of them is also in Roger, onstage, offstage, everywhere he went, with everyone he met. Which gave him the aura of rare, generous-spirited, extraordinary humanity." Well, that's Roger.

It takes no time at all to tell you about how extraordinary I am. Quite simply, I'm extraordinarily *lucky* to be the man Roger Rees fell in love with. He is my teacher, my mentor, my friend, my champion. The man without whose love, my life would be, as Trevor said, a lesser, smaller, darker thing.

For all these years, every time I sit next to Roger, I'm breathless. Our marriage is like the plot of the best play I could ever conceive.

I must admit, before I met Roger—that's to say, before I was twenty-five years old—I didn't know much about love. I had yet to find it, yet to capture it for myself. And I'd had many moments in my life where I'd told myself love wasn't real, or wasn't going to happen to me because I'm gay, or that love fades away after some initial wild spark.

I talked for a couple of hours with Cantor Garfein on Saturday. Roger had just died. I felt dead inside. But I started talking about Roger and I could hear myself come alive.

With every nuance and fragment and twist and turn I could recall of my years with Rog, I felt in my posture, I heard in my voice, what real live love looks and sounds like. All-consuming, tender, passionate, ridiculous, intimate, and so very, very deep. And yes, extraordinary.

Being with Roger every day these last nine months— months that were monstrously challenging for him and me—I've seen how hard he fights and how hard I've fought for him—and with him. Every day and night with him. I've seen how interwoven the two of us truly are. I've seen how much more we loved each other than even I appreciated before the disease came into our lives.

But that's nothing compared to the past two days. Seeing the overwhelming outpouring of love and heartbreak from literally thousands of people all over the world, and in the course of just one weekend—people who knew Roger well and others who admired him from afar—makes me realize that our love story is one for the ages. Inspiring and never-ending and larger than anything I could ever have imagined until now.

My extraordinary husband is gone.

Which, on this July afternoon, makes perfect sense of his favorite sonnet:

Shall I compare thee to a summer's day?
Thou art more lovely and more temperate;
Rough winds do shake the darling buds of May,
And summer's lease hath all too short a date.
Sometime too hot the eye of heaven shines,
And often is his gold complexion dimm'd,
And every fair from fair sometime declines—
By chance or nature's changing course untrimm'd.
But thy eternal summer shall not fade,
Nor lose possession of that fair thou owest;
Nor shall death brag thou wander'st in his shade,
When in eternal lines to time thou growest.
So long as men can breathe or eyes can see,
So long lives this and this gives life to thee.

NOTHING GOLD CAN STAY

YESTERDAY, JULY 13, 2015, we held a small gathering of family and friends at a funeral chapel in New York. At least, that was the plan. By the time the service was scheduled to begin, the funeral director was in the hallway outside the chapel, telling us with no little urgency that "we are breaking all the fire laws; there are just *way* too many people here. We have to start. We have to start so we can finish so we can get all these people out of here!"

However, our cantor, the magnificent Rebecca Garfein, very calmly explained we needed another moment, and the few of us in the room—the immediate family—joined hands in a circle and gently prayed for Roger. And if Rome was burning, so be it.

Rome, of course, wasn't burning at all. It was just a bit overcrowded, like every other place worth being in New York. We thank you, both of us together, for turning out on such short notice and in such heartwarming numbers.

I had no idea how crowded the room was until I got up to speak, and turned to face the room for the first time.

Ian McKellen, the man among us who knew Roger longest—fifty years—was there, representing, as he put it, Roger's pre-New York life, and the multitude of British friends and colleagues. Trevor Nunn sent me the most beautiful e-mail in the morning; enough time for me to include a few sentences in my eulogy. Michael Codron, producer and friend, sent a lovely message. Cameron Mackintosh reached out as well. Harriet Walter, who we saw at Columbus Circle only a couple of months ago, wrote. Finty Williams, Judi Dench's wonderful kid and Roger's chum, checked in for her and for Jude. Richard Cottrell, who knew Rog before he was an actor and Richard was a director, wrote me. Greg Doran, artistic director of the RSC did, too. David Threlfall, Suzanne Bertish, Edward Petherbridge, Patrick Stewart—brilliant actors who love Rog through and through—have all written me the most extraordinary messages. So Sir Ian had many friends from the old days standing behind him.

Roger's newer days were represented by pals from my old agency, Serino Coyne; stage managers and cast members from *The Visit, Something Rotten, Dog and Pony,* and *Peter and the Starcatcher*; from Disney Theatrical Productions, from 321 Management, 101 Productions, Dodger Theatricals; and *Jersey Boys*; Joe Benincasa from The Actors Fund; and producers like Tom Schumacher, Peter Schneider, David Stone, Michael David, Lauren Mitchell, Ed Strong, Sally Morse, Stuart Oken, Tom Kirdahy, Catherine Schreiber, Tom Smedes, Greg Schaffert, and Sandy Block. Authors of note like Tim Federle and Kate Wetherhead. Old friends like Mark Linn-Baker, Christa Justus, Brian Hurley and Kristine Nielsen, Bebe Neuwirth and Joel Grey, Julie Taymor and Dana Ivey. New friends like Chita Rivera and Terrence McNally and President Obama. Okay, so President Obama is a slight exaggeration. It's show business, folks.

And then, of course, the circle of our family. My astonishing parents, Roz and Harold. Auntie Elaine and Uncle Arne, and cousin Scott. Our beautiful niece, Jennifer, and her husband, Eric Gatz. Our legendary nephew, Jeremy. Our incomparable sister-in-law, JoAnn. Our heroic brother, Michael. Their best friends, the Brochsteins, the Rabinowitzes, the Helds, the Freifelds—all of whom adopted Roger as family. My best friend, Nancy Coyne, her daughter, Kate, and their men, Steve Karmen and Ron Martucci. Our lodestones, the

Brickmans, en famille. I could hear Roger asking me, "What are all these people doing here? Did something happen?" He'd never believe so many people had shown up for him. Neither could I. That's why we didn't pick the largest chapel. It seemed impossibly large on Saturday, though we would have filled it easily. I'm only glad I didn't insist on the smallest chapel, which was my idiotic suggestion. (You know the expression "First idea, best idea"? Sometimes not so much.)

Cantor Garfein spoke about Roger and his life with real affection and understanding, and her words are still singing in my ears. My brother got up and scored some big laughs, which was somewhat irritating, since I made it very clear that I would be following him. By the time I got to the microphone, I was so numb, all I can remember is a little sign on the podium that said, RABBIS—DON'T FORGET TO LEAN INTO THE MIC. I hope I leaned in.

Actually, I remember one thing. Roger's favorite of Shakespeare's sonnets, No. 18: "Shall I compare thee to a summer's day?" takes on special relevance when spoken on a broiling hot July afternoon. And the couplet that ends this sonnet—well, perhaps two of the most perfect lines ever written by the hand of man:

> So long as men can breathe and eyes can see,
> So long lives this, and this gives life to thee.

Very hard to say aloud to my darling boy, in front of so many people, and without him smacking me on the arm and saying, "Get on." The rest was not silence—but a blur.

The service was very short and achingly sweet. When it was over, we got to give quick hugs to everyone on the way back out into the summer's day.

I stayed behind for one final look at Rog in his suit and tie. My sweet prince. My champion. My love. He didn't really need the suit and tie. All he needed was a few odd props, whatever was laying around, and easily at hand. And then he'd be ready to make a play happen out of thin air. I think that's what he must be doing now. I just wish I was with him to see it.

About sixty or seventy people found their way over to our place for the traditional Jewish shiva to begin. Lots of people. Lots of food. Cantor Garfein, just before sundown, led us in the mourner's kaddish, and we lit a candle for Rog.

There was a beautiful sunset. Roger loved standing on the terrace at such times, watching the light change moment by moment. We'd stand together, and say aloud one of our favorite non-Shakespeare poems. It's by Robert Frost, and he wrote it about dawn, but we always like to say it at sunset.

Nature's first green is gold,
Her hardest hue to hold.
Her early leaf's a flower;
But only so an hour.
The leaf subsides to leaf.
So Eden sank to grief.
So dawn goes down to day.
Nothing gold can stay.

Nothing gold can stay.

So . . . here we are—two fleeting shadows who had a brief time together—signing off now with lots of love to every one of you, from both of us.

God bless.
Rog and Rick

DIMMING THE LIGHTS

I THOUGHT I'D STOP THESE REPORTS, but last night on West Forty-Fifth Street, in the gloaming—our favorite time of day, when Broadway gets ready for showtime—several friends and a handful of strangers asked me to continue sending out messages. "They really help," someone said. And so . . .

Last night, the lights of Broadway were dimmed in Roger's honor. This is not, sadly, a rare occurrence these days. People are leaving us all the time. But this is the first time I witnessed the new LED-screen marquees personalized in tribute to the person being honored.

The whole event of it was very meaningful, albeit brief. Hundreds of people jammed the street, all in the vicinity of the Schoenfeld Theatre, formerly called the Plymouth. When it was the Plymouth in 1981, *Nicholas Nickleby* played there for fourteen weeks, and no one who saw it would ever be the same.

I've never seen anything like it—but I've never known anyone like Rog. I don't think he ever knew he was so loved by so many. I certainly had no idea until this weekend, when I started hearing from people all over the world. Hundreds of them, then thousands. One thing I do know is that Rog was loved by someone whom he loved just as much. So last night, I was overwhelmed for both of us, and proud for both of us. Somewhere along the way, just living our lives, it seems as though we became a couple whose existence, as a couple, delighted and reassured and inspired. Who knew?

Thanks, then, from both of us, to everyone who was present—from Phil Smith and Bob Wankel, the leaders of the Shubert Organization, who hosted my family, to Liz McCann and Nelle Nugent, the first producers Roger ever knew in New York—both of them living legends; Jordan Roth and Paul Libin from Jujamcyn; Joe Benincasa, head of The Actors Fund; Michael David and Lauren Mitchell; Stuart and Carol Oken; William Ivey Long, my Yale pal; Joe Machota, my amazing agent and friend; cast members from a half dozen Broadway shows; the crème de la crème of Broadway press agents and managers; Alan Siegel, Michael Moore, and Gary Gersh, Roger's reps and dearest friends. And my family and inner circle, who finally got to meet the people they've been hearing me jabber about for years and years and years and years and years.

After a spontaneous ovation, which went on for what seemed like minutes, a bunch of us—maybe fifty people—walked over to The Glass House, a bar where Rog and I would hang out almost every night after *Peter and the Starcatcher*. There we met up with more Broadway folks, all of whom had extraordinary things to say about Rog, and wonderful stories to tell. It's the stories that will help Rog live on, I can feel it. It's how we'll conjure him—by recounting the tales of how he made the world better, happier, and more fun for the rest of us.

Before they become frozen in aspic, I thought I'd share one man's recollection, because he's a great guy and a journalist, so his affection for Rog is leavened with literary flair.

His name is Patrick Pacheco. We were introduced years ago by our mutual friend, Peter Schneider.

But long before I met him, I knew his byline. Years and years ago, when all the other boys were trying to steal *Playboy* magazine from the five-and-dime store on the corner, I was trying to get a look at *After Dark* magazine. It was a theater mag with a certain homoerotic bent, and I thought that if I could just touch an edition, I might one day become a Broadway actor.

Pacheco wrote for *After Dark*. That's the first place I ever saw his name with any regularity. Turns out he did a feature on Roger in 1975. And yesterday, he wrote this tribute, quoting liberally from that earlier piece. I'm reprinting it here for your delectation. Because it is delectable.

Portrait of the Artist as a Young Man
by Patrick Pacheco / July 15, 2015

The general public knew Roger Rees best for his television roles as Robin Colcord in *Cheers* and Lord John Marbury in *The West Wing*. But the Welsh-born actor, who died on July 10 at the age of 71, was, at heart, a theater animal. That lifelong commitment to the stage will be acknowledged on July 15 when the lights of the Broadway theaters will be dimmed in his honor.

Rees lit up the stage with his radiant talent, most notably in the title role of the Royal Shakespeare Company's epic 1981 production of *The Life and Adventures of Nicholas Nickleby*, for which he won the Tony Award. He was nominated twice more, in a revival of Cocteau's *Indiscretions*, opposite Jude Law and Kathleen Turner, and again as co-director with Alex Timbers of the wildly inventive *Peter and the Starcatcher*. His last appearance on Broadway was two months ago in *The Visit*, opposite Chita Rivera.

I'd had the privilege of meeting Rees in early 1975, six years before his star turn in *Nicholas Nickleby*, when he made his Broadway debut in the RSC's production of Dion Boucicault's *London Assurance*. I was a callow reporter at *After Dark* magazine and he was one of my first interviews when we met on a wintry night at a midtown Manhattan restaurant, the Monk's Inn, where the waiters were dressed in habits and cowls.

Then all of thirty, with a thick dark mane of hair setting off his handsome features, Rees was idealistic, charming, and, to this inexperienced reporter, very English in his elegant three-piece suit and crisp white shirt. When our waiter accidentally stained that shirt while pouring a bottle of wine, Rees was all apologies as though it were his fault. After the young man departed, the actor quipped, "I suppose you could get defrocked for that."

Self-deprecating and modest, Rees spoke of the theater

as a refuge from an isolated and lonely boyhood in which he found himself hard-pressed to join in the activities of his school mates. So it was a boon when this son of a policeman was chosen to sing a solo—"Once in Royal David's City"—at the Christmas service at Southwark Cathedral. But as the boy watched the throngs filing into the church, he turned on his heels and ran away, leaving a frantic choirmaster to find a substitute. "I wanted to do it so much that somehow I felt compelled to flee," he recalled then. "Sounds strange, doesn't it?"

A couple of decades later, Rees was performing with the RSC in *The Taming of the Shrew* in Japan when an earthquake struck and the audience fled the theater in panic. The actors remained rooted on stage. "Since none of us had ever been in an earthquake before, we didn't know quite what to do," he said. "So we just continued playing the scene. After the initial shock, the audience came filing back in."

By that time, Rees had become so enamored of the stage that wild horses, much less an earthquake, couldn't have pried him from it. But it had not been easy. He was an aspiring painter, then enrolled in London's Slade School of Fine Art, when his father died suddenly and he dropped out to care for his family. He took odd jobs, including spending one Christmas waist-deep in mud helping to build the Victoria line underground. It was while Rees was painting scenery for Arthur Lane, one of the last of the great British actor-managers, that the impresario induced him to make his stage debut in Stanley Houghton's *Hindle Wakes*. He'd found a home. "There's something very fine and lucid and rich in this tradition of the English actor," he said. "A richness of observation and character that you find in Rembrandt paintings and Bruegel crowd scenes, and I'm terribly grateful to Arthur that I was able to share in some part of it."

Auditions for the RSC followed. The first one was a disaster. "They said my voice was terrible, nervous, and spotty, and that I must go away and learn how to use it properly," said Rees. "I must admit I was rather agape since I had never thought about making my voice better. I thought acting was just going on and remembering all of one's lines."

Though it would be several years later that Rees would return to the United States, eventually making it his home and taking citizenship, he then expressed an admiration for the American theater. "There's a tough, gritty professionalism that is very impressive . . . that intense pressure to achieve, to be professional," he said. "On the other hand, the English tend to applaud a certain kind of amateurishness. The fool is embraced because there is a recognition of silliness there that allows a person to keep his ambitions and desires at a certain distance. Just being in the race is enough."

Rees then expressed the desire to safeguard that "silliness" within himself—"the ability to let go of things that one prizes very much without a sense of loss." He lifted the sleeve of his black suit jacket to reveal a bright yellow cat collar. "I wear this to remind me."

When the conversation turned to his personal life, Rees said that he been nearly married twice and now lived in his London home with neighbors upstairs and a girlfriend and cat downstairs. If he hadn't found the right girl it is probably because seven years after our interview he would find the right boy, a handsome young writer, Rick Elice, who would become his husband. For the next thirty-odd years, they'd be one of Broadway's most popular, devoted, and successful couples. They'd collaborate on a mystery, *Double Double*, before Elice would go on to co-write *Jersey Boys* and *The Addams Family* with Marshall Brickman. Rees would take on the role of Gomez in the latter and then the two would collaborate once more on *Peter and the Starcatcher* to much acclaim.

That brilliant future lay well ahead of the actor when we closed down the Monk's Inn on that winter night. The waiters had taken off their habits by then and were shooting glances in our direction when Rees opened his arms expansively and said, "Oh, I want to do so much! I really don't approve of people going off to islands. I suppose I have this relenting Christian image of coping with all the hassles and obstacles of daily life with taxi strikes and fuel shortages, disappointments and heartaches, taking up your cross to bear and setting out like John Bunyan's Pilgrim to accomplish what you have to do."

Roger Rees, May 5, 1944–July 10, 2015. Well done, pilgrim, and farewell.

Thank you, Patrick.
Lots of love to everyone,
Rick

WORDS OF WISDOM

SO MANY PEOPLE ARE CLAMORING to keep these reports going. So here I am again.

Next week, they'll take a different turn, because next week, with a few friends like Christian Borle and John Sanders and Corey Cott and Jerry Mitchell and Lon Hoyt, and some other outrageously talented people, I'm going to spend a scant twenty-nine hours trying to see if a story that Roger and I talked about can take wing as a show. It's got a particularly British point of view, you might say. But since it's written by a Yank, me, the Brit quotient is affectionate without being alienating (I hope). Roger will be giving me notes; this time however, we'll save on paper. He'll just look at me sternly, and lovingly tell me, "Better, yes it's better. But better isn't the same as good." More of that anon.

Roger surrounded/British Art Institute, New Haven, February 2012

In order to keep the reports going 'til then, and to satisfy what has grown into a transatlantic craving for Reesiana, I'm going to share with you something extraordinary written a couple of hundred years ago by an American icon who was, not incidentally, a Franco- and Anglophile for a large part of his life, until events overtook him. This was sent to me by the ever-young Freddie and Myrna Gershon, and it feels like it could have been written this week, expressly for us. Which is, of course, the secret of all truly great writing.

First, let me set the stage, in this case, the one at the Apollo Theatre on Shaftesbury Avenue in London:

Roger, preparing for his one-man show, What You Will/*Apollo Theatre, September 2012*

We have lost a most dear and valuable friend. But it is the Will of God and nature that these mortal bodies be laid aside when the soul is to enter into real life. This is rather an embryo state, a preparation for living. A man is not completely born until he be dead. Why then should we grieve that a new child is born among the immortals, a new member added to their happy society.

We are spirits. That bodies should be lent us, while they can afford us pleasure, assist us in acquiring knowledge, or in doing good to our fellow creatures, is a kind and benevolent act of God. When they become unfit for these purposes, and afford us pain instead of pleasure, instead of an aid become an encumbrance, and answer none of the intentions for which they were given, it is equally kind and benevolent that a way is provided by which we may get rid of them. Death is that way.

We ourselves occasionally choose a partial death. A mangled, painful limb which cannot be restored, we willingly cut off. He who plucks out a tooth parts with it freely, since the pain goes with it. He who quits the whole body, parts at once with all pains and possibilities of diseases which it was capable of making him suffer.

Our friend and we are invited abroad on a party of pleasure which is to last forever. His chair was ready first, and he is gone before us. We could not all conveniently start together. But why should you and I be grieved at this, since we are soon to follow, and know just where to find him.

—Benjamin Franklin

Roger's disease is no longer keeping him from doing what he loved so much. He beat it in April. It stopped him in May. He pushed it aside last Friday night. And now, and now, and now. . . .

I pray, tonight, he's back onstage, some other stage, doing what he loved most to do, being what he loved most to be. Flowers strewn.

I can see him there, and I'm cheering for him. I'm clapping my hands raw. You, too. Try it for us, won't you? Think about him, friends. Stand up for him, speak of him. And Roger will endure.

More soon.
xRick

Roger, at the curtain call for The Visit
on opening night, April 23, 2015

MARSHALL BRICKMAN
A Speech at Roger's Memorial, New Amsterdam Theatre, September 21, 2015

The enduring image I have of Roger is not, as you might expect, of his Astrov in *Uncle Vanya*; or Henry in *The Real Thing*, or Malcolm in *Macbeth*, or Hamlet, or Robin Colcord in *Cheers*, or Lord John Marbury in *West Wing*, or even as the Sheriff of Rottingham in *Robin Hood: Men in Tights*. The image that endures for me is from about twenty-five years ago—Nina and I had a house in Montauk, and Rick and Roger had come for the weekend. And even before they had unpacked, Roger disappeared and then emerged from the cellar with a shovel and a trowel and a pair of work gloves, and suddenly there was Nicholas Nickleby on his knees digging and arranging, and by the time they left a few days later, we had a garden.

And that garden—for as long as we had the house, which was many years—produced thyme, tarragon and tomatoes, and roses and tulips. That was Roger. Quietly, without fanfare, he always left behind something of himself. A gift that kept giving and giving and giving.

I'm probably going to get this wrong, but Saint Thomas Aquinas—if I may be permitted to reference a goy icon—Thomas, Saint Tom, caught in some difficult paradox about the perfection of God, decided that we mortals, imperfect as we are, could not possibly conceive of perfection. Well, as a Jew, and someone who had the opportunity to see the man close-up, I beg to differ. If there ever was a perfect thing, Roger was it.

Roger was, in fact, a perfect person. He was gifted beyond comprehension. He was dazzlingly beautiful. He had perfect hair. His mouth and nose also were not chopped liver. You never caught him acting, especially when he was acting. His devotion to Rick, and their shared faith in each other, was an absolute definition of faith itself. He was kind, he was empathetic, he was generous and funny and dependable. And in a career spanning fifty years, he never missed a performance. I'll say that again: in a fifty-year career, Rog never missed a performance. He was, in fact, the anti-Liza.

In addition to his theatrical accomplishments, he gave our kids a rounded education without even knowing it. Back in the late eighties, we had pretty strict rules about what Sophie and Jessica Brickman, aged four and eight respectively, could and could not watch on television. It was our belief that *Sesame Street* did not teach children to read and count. What it did was to teach children to watch television.

What they were allowed to watch, our kids, was the RSC production of *The Life and Adventures of Nicholas Nickleby*. This was available, if you recall, on nine one-hour VHS tapes.

We must have worn out half a dozen copies by the time the girls were in high school. The nine tapes cost back then about fifty bucks. The combined tuition of both girls for four years was about two hundred thousand dollars. Which, do you think, gave them a better education? An appreciation of what it is to be a human being. The importance of family and loyalty. A better understanding of social injustice. And the beauty of language spoken by a master in a role he was born to play.

I am a rational man. For the most part, I believe in things that can be proven and duplicated. But in Roger's case, I'll make an exception. This may be cold comfort for Rick, but for the rest of us, Roger isn't really gone. A verb has changed, that's all. Present tense to past perfect. Everything else remains, informs, and enlightens us, makes us better. The work, the unforgettable performances, the lives he changed, his brief but powerful presence on earth.

Roger was born Welsh but embraced many things British, among them a framed poster that hangs on their library wall, suggesting to the populace how they might deal with catastrophe. KEEP CALM, it says. KEEP CALM AND CARRY ON. Easier said than done.

But under the circumstances, pretty good advice.

WHY CAN'T I DREAM?

WITH THE HELP OF MY BROTHER AND SISTER-IN-LAW,
I've put the apartment back to something like what it was before. It
feels like a time capsule now—I don't have it in me to do anything but
restore. Nothing new to sit on, no new art to look at, only the comfort
of the utterly familiar. It is what's left.

We spent most of the day yesterday organizing thank-you cards
for everybody—I'll try to get them out soon, but I have to get a couple
hundred stamps first. We'll see how that goes.

On Friday, I went to my therapist, Dr. Weiss, and said I was upset
that I hadn't yet dreamed of Rog. My dreams are usually so vivid, and I
haven't been dreaming at all—or at least not aware of having dreamed.
My sleep feels more like a blackout, probably because, until last week,
I hadn't really slept at all since February. The dread that had been a
daily companion ("Good morning, heartache—sit down . . .") while
Roger was sick and getting sicker is gone, replaced by sadness. Sadness
sucks, but it's a heckuva lot better than dread. "What does it mean, that

I'm not able to dream of Rog?" I
asked her. Dr. Weiss suggested it
needn't mean anything. Rational,
but not satisfying.

Late Friday night, Susan
Haskins and Michael Riedel
rebroadcast a *Theater Talk* show
on PBS, in which I make Roger
really uncomfortable on-camera
while I describe how much writers,
directors, and actors adore him,
and how lucky I am to be the man
who shares his life. I remember

61

the day we taped this show, wondering if I would have the nerve to go through with my scheme. Obama had just "evolved" on the subject of marriage equality; Roger and I had been married for less than a year, but it still wasn't legal if we crossed the Hudson River into New Jersey. So I decided to stop talking about theater and say some personal things about Roger, because I wanted people to see two men in love, to demystify it, to honor it. He was mortified. I wasn't very good—my heart was pounding out of my chest—but I'm so glad I said what I said publicly, so that I don't now regret missing the chance.

Now it's Sunday morning, and Roger still hasn't stopped by in my unconscious or my subconscious or my sub-unconscious to say, *hello, everything's okay, don't worry, get on with it.* Throughout these early days of mourning, these long days of shifting one's weight, everything seems so fraught with meaning (Dr. Weiss's advice notwithstanding). Tikkun olam: Does it mean something, not dreaming? Does everything acquire an eerie, beyond-the-grave significance now that Rog is gone? Is he really gone? What if, maybe, he's trying to reach me? In a world where there is no proof about anything, where there's no such thing as absolute surety, is maybe good enough? Is Dr. Weiss correct; is it better, wiser, truer to accept what's happened and get back to living, even if this is all living is going to be? And if this is all there is, isn't it better to just go back to sleep, to sleep, perchance to dream of Rog?

And speaking of Hamlet . . .

Roger as Hamlet in 1984

These are the thoughts meandering through my head this morning, after watching *On Stage* on NY1, during which Donna Karger, the show's intrepid host, presented a very sweet tribute to Roger.

Then I heard something: the sound of something falling in the other room.

I went in to investigate. The sun glinted off something on the floor. Something on the marble hearth in front of the fireplace. What was it?

It was a small metal square, silver colored, with five words engraved: AMERICAN THEATRE WING TONY AWARD. It had fallen off of Roger's Tony (for *Nicholas Nickleby* in 1982). It had never fallen off before. I held it in my hand, and I started to laugh. "You *are* here! Hello, baby! Hello, my love!" I ran to Roger's supply closet and got some double-sided tape and reaffixed the plaque. Because I knew, I *knew* that this was Rog saying hello.

You see, the Tony sits on the mantel in our office with some other stuff we've managed to win for this or that, but it's not close to the edge, or precarious in any way. It's just sitting there in a lineup, minding its own business. Until this morning at 9:45 a.m., when, all of a sudden, it popped its cork.

Tell me I'm crazy. But I'm a believer. Rog passed through. And I'm glad I was home when he did. Either that, or it's the heat and I need to get out of the sun. I can go either way. But I suspect our mischievous friend Mister Rees was "having a go."

It might have been Roger flying off to London, where he had hoped to be present at Richard Pasco's memorial service at the Actors' Church in Covent Garden. Dickie Pasco was a great mentor to Rog, and he so wanted to be there today—to join with his beloved gang of RSC mates, packing into the church to honor one of The Greats.

Richard Pasco,
1926–2014

I hope Rog made it there after all, and much love to Barbara Leigh-Hunt and everyone supporting her, from Roger and me. Bravo, Dickie!

Enjoy the balmy night, dear Report reader—and if you hear anything clattering in the other room tonight, it might just be Rog and Richard Pasco being a bit naughty.

God bless and lots of love,
Rick

TWENTY-NINE-HOUR WEEK

I'M WRITING YOU FROM THE FORMER Snapple Theater Center, stripped of its Snapple signage but still home of *The Fantasticks* and *Perfect Crime*—the longest-running musical and play in New York. The latter was written by a Yale Drama School guy who was a wonderful, smart, and rangy actor, Warren Manzi.

It's in this building that I'm engaged in a twenty-nine-hour week on a new musical. I think we're in hour nine. Twenty to go. At the end of which, we'll have a better sense of our show.

It's very early and the actors (or as Roger would describe them, "the pampered lovelies") have yet to arrive. I wanted to come early because to come early is to beat the worst of the morning heat, which on days like today, needs to be beaten at all costs. Or at least the cost of a few more minutes at home. And it's good to be away from home on these days, because everything there speaks of Rog.

Only, everything here speaks of Rog, too. The empty, wonderfully shabby room. The metal folding chairs. The sagging worktables. The recycle bin. The printer brought in by the stage managers.

Dog and Pony at The Old Globe in San Diego, May 2014. Rog is shown colluding with Anjee Nero, the production stage manager. Behind him is Lisa Shriver, who's choreographing Nicole Parker and Jon Patrick Walker.

(Arthur Laurents once told me that writing for the theater is almost entirely rewriting. I've always taken that to heart . . . to a fault I'm sure. Roger would say, "Let them have another go before you change it around." I'd say, "I just want them to be happy." And he'd say, "Then give them a chance.")

Being in a rehearsal room, pregnant with possibility—oh yeah, that's heaven for us. Much more likely for Rog to be here than anywhere, unless it's a rehearsal room on Forty-Second Street, or in Stratford-upon-Avon, or in a basement in San Diego, or even the upstairs lounge in a Broadway theater.

Alex Timbers (standing, right) and Rog (sitting by Alex's feet) giving notes to the original Broadway cast of Peter and the Starcatcher *at the Brooks Atkinson Theatre, March 2012*

The actors are here now, including our pal Christian Borle, whose booted feet you can see on the left in the photo above. The director (Jerry Mitchell), the music director (Lon Hoyt), stage managers and cast, all in top form, all in place, ready to start the day. All of 'em getting set to make something out of nothing, maybe even something wonderful. To give it their best shot. And I get to watch. I get to rewrite. I get to be. I'm so happy, Rog. I'm in the room where it happens. And I can feel you, husband, looking over my shoulder. Perfection, you always said, is a moving point. But could you not move, just for a bit? Hold still, my love, and stay with me.

Speaking of San Diego, I got a letter, a rather remarkable one, from Jack O'Brien last night. Jack is an original in every way that's important. When Jack was running San Diego's much-loved Old Globe theater, he invited Rog to direct some plays over the years. These days our apartment in New York is right across the street from Jack's building, so we're proper neighbors, and right neighborly, too. There's one paragraph I'd like to share from Jack's letter, because it expresses so well what so many of you have written and continue to write about Rog:

You loved him most, and most consistently, but we loved him as well. Literally everyone in Roger's path, in his wake, was swept up with his enthusiasm, his wit, his profound generosity of spirit. Loss is as hideous as it is inevitable across the board, but some losses count more than others—they just do. Roger's is one of those. If "each man's death diminishes me," then this one has reduced us to rubble. There will never be another like him.

Thank you, Jack.

Let me pay attention to rehearsal now, and I'll be in touch again tomorrow.

Lots of love to everyone,
Rick

PASTURES GREEN

DANA IVEY IS THE GIFTED ACTRESS and world traveler with whom Rog was lucky enough to act on occasion . . .

Dana Ivey and Roger in The Uneasy Chair/*Playwrights Horizons, New York, 1998*

. . . and to direct on occasion.

Dana Ivey in The Rivals, *directed by Roger / Williamstown Theatre Festival, Massachusetts, 1998*

Dana wrote me the other day. She included an e-mail thread in which a fellow wrote about the RSC season in 1984–85 that included Antony Sher as Richard III, Ken Branagh as Henry V, Roger Rees as Hamlet, and Ken and Roger together in *Love's Labour's Lost.*

Kenneth Branagh as Navarre and Roger as Berowne in Love's Labour's Lost */ RSC 1984*

In the aforementioned e-mail thread, the gentleman explained that he almost met Roger in 1984 in Stratford-upon-Avon after seeing Roger play Hamlet, and went to the Dirty Duck (the local pub across from the RSC main-stage) with Ken Branagh (who played Laertes) and Frances Barber (who played Ophelia). But Roger didn't want to come.

I wrote back to Dana that Roger had only just stopped drinking when he went to Stratford that season. He'd had a couple of "incidents," culminating in one life-altering interaction with the local constabulary in South London who knocked him up (as they say) one morning. Roger came bleary-eyed to the front door, and the policeman said, "We've removed your car from the bridge. Here's the address where you can go round to retrieve it."

Roger didn't know what the policeman was talking about. "What bridge?" he asked. "The Prince Albert Bridge," the cop said.

"My car was on Prince Albert Bridge?"

"Only partly, I'm afraid. The front wheels were more off than on."

Rog had no recollection of nearly driving off the bridge, nor did he recall leaving his car, nor could he understand how he ended up home and in bed. It was all a blank. That was the wake-up call he needed, and that was the day he stopped drinking.

And once Rog stopped drinking, he just stopped. He didn't believe in AA (which in England, at any rate, is what the AAA is here). Point is, no twelve-step program for our Rog. He was British to the bone, and simply stopped.

A few weeks later, he began rehearsals for *Hamlet*.

*Roger as Hamlet;
RSC, 1984*

Roger, being newly on the wagon, decided to forsake visits to the Dirty Duck—the site of so many nightly drunks and debauches for so many years. The Duck was quite off his calendar. And would stay off. "Too hard to play Hamlet and drink," he firmly believed. Even after he'd played his 140-odd performances of the great Dane in Stratford and, later, in London, he still never touched a drop. And hasn't for thirty years.

Meanwhile, thirty years later, this photo was taken on October 22, 2014, a mere six days after Roger's first brain surgery last fall. He was two days back home, and you can't see the back of his head, which had a ten-inch horseshoe-shaped scar with about a hundred staples in it. While Rog was in the hospital, a fan had sent him a T-shirt with his RSC Hamlet poster silk-screened on it. Rog asked me to take this photo of him wearing the T-shirt, holding his Yorick skull (which he kept all these years), to send back to the fan, autographed, of course.

Does this look like a man who, six days earlier, had a surgeon carving a tumor out of his brain? Is accommodating a fan something a man would do after being told he had brain cancer? Yes, if the man is Roger Rees. He never felt sorry for himself, he never withdrew, he never shook his fist at the sky, and he never even chose to "think positive." He just *was* positive, always and forever.

One more thought about why Roger didn't go across the road with Ken and Frances to the Dirty Duck. It occurs to me that maybe I was in Stratford that night. I was there a lot. I saw *Hamlet* so many times, I made a blanket out of all my ticket stubs. Not a throw, mind you—a proper blanket. It's quite possible I was in Stratford that night, and Roger just wanted to come home with me.

Home, during the season Roger played Hamlet and Berowne, was a large, mostly empty house on Welcombe Road that belonged to Trevor Nunn, who was still co-artistic director of the RSC, though not in Stratford full-time. The house was a sprawling brick pile that backed onto a pasture. Every evening, cows would lope up the hill to the fence that divided Trevor's yard from the pasture. I loved those cows, and when I was there, I'd make Rog a bit of dinner before he'd head off to the theater, and I'd stay behind, take the leftovers out back, and feed the cows. Pretty soon, I'd named the ones that were super-friendly (or super-hungry)—their willingness to eat what I gave them the only metric I had for true human-bovine friendship. On Roger's nights off (there were four plays in rep and Rog appeared in just two of them), we'd feed the cows together. I have no pictures of the cows in Stratford, or of the house on Welcombe Road.

Tom (with bucket) and Rog (with Holden, Tom and Matt's dachshund, and Roger's chum)

But . . . years and years later, our friends Matthew White and Tom Schumacher started to tend some cows of their own up in Hillsdale, New York. Every time Rog and I go up there, one of the first orders of business is Tom taking Rog down to feed the cows.

I'll usually go along, hoping to overcome my Semitic pheromonal aversions to insects and livestock . . .

. . . and fail utterly—*udderly*, even. Oy.

But every time that Tom, Rog, and I head down to Tom's barn and call the cows over for a meal, I think about that pasture behind Trevor's house on Welcombe Road in Stratford.

And every time we had the pleasure of being up at Tom and Matt's place, Rog always read some Shakespeare aloud. Because he was thinking of the Stratford pasture, too.

The pasture in Stratford is still there. The cows and Rog are gone. Somehow, I guess that's the way of the world.

Share your food. Feed the animals. Keep the grass fertilized. And eventually, move over so someone else can use the pasture.

Lots of love to everyone,
Rick

PS: Here's an old card I just came across, a celebratory note when we stopped crossing oceans to see each other and moved in together. Roger first promised me it would happen, that we would actually live together, the first time I visited him in Stratford, at Trevor Nunn's house on Welcombe Road.

Me and Rog celebrating cohabitation with exclamation points!

SAVE THE DATE

YESTERDAY, I STOOD ON THE CORNER of Fiftieth Street
and Eighth Avenue with my pal, Christian Borle, who'd just given a
couple of dozen actors a master class in showstopping at a workshop
presentation of a musical I've been working on. It's set in a rock-
and-roll club in London called the Bag O' Nails. Rog hung out there
occasionally when he was nineteen and twenty years old. I suddenly
started bawling on the corner, because I couldn't bear the thought of
not being able to tell him how it went.

This morning, I was on the phone with my pal, Nancy Coyne. And
I was still pretty weepy. "I just don't know where to find him," I said to
her. "I keep looking through his stuff, through his clothes, through his
plants on the terrace."

This morning, I found a new sweet pea blooming—from seeds
planted by Rog on his birthday, May 5. I took a picture the way I always
do when he's not home, so I can send it to him—and then I realized I
don't know where to send it. And it's the sweetest little sweet pea.

Rog loved his terrace garden, and we'd be out there with coffee and
the paper every morning in good weather.

Like every good gardener, Rog was as
interested in the weeds as in the flowers.
We have some very robust ones blooming
now, especially an English weed called
tansy. It's one of the only things hardy
enough to come back each year, after the
harshness of winter. Rog knew even the
Latin names of all these plants that I now
tend for him.

I'm happy to be working on plays,
working in that garden, too, as it were,

but moving forward is really hard. I just keep hoping to put one foot in front of the other; that's about all I'm capable of at the moment. Someone said, "How are you supposed to move forward without your arms or legs?" That sounds about right.

Had a lot of time to get used to the idea of life without my love, but the reality of it is much tougher than I imagined. The terror and rage at the cruelty of Roger's disease has been replaced by the consuming sorrow of his absence. I miss my arms and legs, my heart and soul. So yes, I'm keeping busy. But it's like watching the world from down the bottom of a deep, dark well.

But I digress. . . .

Our friend, Kate Burton, who just started performances of *Cymbeline* in Central Park this week, wrote me this the other day:

> **I laugh every single time you write "but I digress" . . . and the blessed heartache . . . which is so important for all of us as we are all so heartbroken . . . and yes, sitting in rehearsal at the Delacorte in the searing 90-degree heat has been the worst of times and the best of times and I am thinking of Roger in the Beresford and in *Hamlet* and in *Nicholas Nickleby*, and of the Elizabethan and Jacobean players at The Globe always doing their shows in the daytime because there was no electricity, and of what Roger said about what it is to be an English actor, and that I am the daughter of such an extraordinary actor who was an influence on Roger as a young man, and that he became such an extraordinary actor . . . and it is all one big circle, isn't it?**

I'm not sure whether Kate knows this: her father passed away while Roger was rehearsing *Hamlet* in Stratford. It was almost twenty years to the day from Richard Burton's last performance as Hamlet on

Broadway. I happened to be with Rog in Stratford that week, and we had the radio on, and that's how we heard the news. And Roger said, "Well, this Hamlet's for him then, isn't it?" Years later, in 2011, Roger was playing in *The Addams Family* at the Lunt-Fontanne Theatre on Broadway, and he occupied the dressing room that Richard Burton had used in 1964, when he played Hamlet on Broadway. So when Kate says it's all "one big circle," she speaks true.

I've digressed again. Allow me to get to the subject of this report:

`September 21, 2015.` That's a Monday, and at 1 p.m. on that particular Monday, at the New Amsterdam Theatre on West Forty-Second Street (where *Aladdin* is currently playing), we're going to celebrate Roger and Roger's life, and you're all invited to come. It's a big honking theater with plenty of seats, so please spread the word: Monday, September 21 at 1 p.m., at the New Am.

It'll be the second limited engagement Roger had on Broadway. The first was in 1981 with *Nicholas Nickleby*.

Although in London three years ago, he played a limited run of his show, *What You Will*, in the West End. He shared the stage with his favorite collaborator, Will Shakespeare.

Tom Schumacher and my friends at Disney Theatrical Productions are making this possible, and it's a great big hug of a gesture and a lot of work, so I'm saying THANK YOU here and everywhere else I can think of.

In the meantime, please save the date. I'll send out more information about the program as it takes shape.

Nicholas Nickleby was eight and a half hours long. *What You Will* was an hour and a half. Roger's memorial will be one hour long.

One brief shining hour—to celebrate our once and future friend, colleague, mentor, love.

We'll see you, I hope, on September 21 at the New Amsterdam Theatre.

Lots of love to everyone,
Rick

Roger with his favorite collaborator

JOHN CAIRD /
A Speech at Roger's Memorial, New Amsterdam Theatre, September 21, 2015

On this very day, thirty-four years ago, Roger Rees and I, together with some sixty or so dearly beloved colleagues from the RSC, were struggling through an extremely slow stagger-through rehearsal of *The Life and Adventures of Nicholas Nickleby* at the Plymouth Theatre, now the Schoenfeld Theatre.

The show was eight and a half hours long. The rehearsal had taken all that day and half the night. We'd all just arrived in New York from England a few days earlier, and we were completely exhausted from the endless technical rehearsals. And the only person who never seemed fatigued or exhausted in any way was Roger. He was always the calm epicenter of the storm. And that was the effect he had on every company he was ever in.

He was the perfect company leader. But he led, seemingly, effortlessly. Quick-witted, funny, generous, and never remotely self-important or egotistical. As an actor, he did what actors always do: he changed himself, of course, to play his roles. But the roles he played were also obliged to become like Roger. He had a centrifugal effect on all the parts he played. And they always seemed to be improved in the process.

Nicholas Nickleby was a wonderful example of this. Dickens doesn't give his actors much to go on with his heroes. So Roger had to *become* Nicholas, while also demanding that Nicholas become like him. With all of Roger's sweetness and strength and wit and nonsense and fun.

Back to thirty-four years ago—the very next day, September 22, was the gypsy run-through. The house was packed to the gunnels with all our Broadway colleagues, none of whom we knew at that point, but I bet there are more than a few people here today who were in that audience.

The first half ran that day from 2 to 6 p.m. There was an

hour's dinner break. The second half ran from 7 p.m. until just before midnight.

At the final curtain call, just after Roger had stood onstage, lifting the nearly frozen orphan boy in his arms and offering him to the audience, the theater erupted into the most rapturous ovation I have ever witnessed.

My codirector, Trevor Nunn, and I were standing in the mezzanine, soaking up the glory, when Roger, ever-generous, waved to us to join the cast onstage. Trevor and I made our way to the stage, and joined the lineup—where we took several breathless bows.

I was holding hands with Trevor on my right and Roger on my left, when out of the corner of my eye, I saw Shirley King, the actress who played Mrs. Kenwigs—a wonderful Welsh actress and a very close friend of Roger's—emerging from the stage left wing, carrying a birthday cake ablaze with candles.

I looked around me, to see whose birthday it might be, and Roger, sensing my bewilderment, squeezed my hand and said, "It's *yours*, you fool!" And it was mine. In my fatigue, I had omitted to remember it was my birthday. I took the cake from Shirley, and I saw Roger's face twinkling at me. This had been his idea. To include my birthday celebration in the curtain call of *Nicholas Nickleby*.

The whole cast and over a thousand Broadway gypsies sang Happy Birthday to me. I don't remember blowing the candles out. I think my tears must have quenched them first.

It was a momentous day for all of us. It changed all our lives, that play. But I've been thinking a lot over the past few days how much more momentous that play and that night turned out to be for Roger than for any of the rest of us.

For it was Roger who became completely enchanted with this city. Almost as if he had come home. Which in many ways, of course, he had. Within a year of *Nicholas Nickleby*, he returned and met his soul mate here, his creative muse and husband, our dear friend and the love of Roger's life, Rick Elice.

A MOTHER'S JOURNEY

THIS REPORT IS A CELEBRATION OF MOTHERS. More specifically, I'd like you to know more about Rog by honoring the relationship he had with my mom, Roz Elice.

Since Roger's own mum passed away in 1989, my mother's been his mother. He loved her a lot, and demonstrated that love a million different ways. Mom loved him right back. When he went into the hospital in June with pneumonia, my mom said she was coming into town to visit him. I suggested it was kind of an arduous trip for her to think about making. She said, "I want to see my son-in-law." She stayed with him in the hospital for three different days over the two weeks he was there. As awful as the whole hospital experience was, and as difficult and exhausting as the two subsequent weeks were, I'll never forget my reaction to hearing my mother say, "I want to see my son-in-law." It wasn't the first time she referred to Roger this way. But my reaction is the same every time she says it. My reaction is joy.

It was quite a road over the years that my mother and Roger traveled, for her to be able to say that. I told this story to Danielle Robinson, who works with Alan Siegel,

JANUARY 1983 90¢

PLAYS & players

INSIDE: LONDON THEATRE CRITICS' POLL: THE BEST OF 1982

Roger and Felicity Kendal in The Real Thing

Roger's longtime manager and best friend in Los Angeles. Danielle came to New York to reminisce with me about Rog. She suggested that I share this story.

It starts with a tribute to Roger's mum, Doris—whom everyone called Lucy. She was the sort of woman Damon Runyon would've called "a right broad."

By now you know that Rog and I met in September 1982 (at the dress rehearsal to *Cats*), had swapped addresses, and started corresponding. He was rehearsing the original production of *The Real Thing* in London with the fabulous Felicity Kendal . . . while I had just started working full-time as a copywriter for Nancy Coyne at what was then called Serino, Coyne & Nappi.

Left to right: Nancy Coyne, me, and Nick Nappi, 1983 (absent: Matthew Serino)

When Roger departed New York after we met, he said to write him, and I did, copiously; what else could I do? I was wildly infatuated. The amazing thing was Rog answered my letters with letters of his own. And photos—because, you know, actors always have photos. For example, here's the photo he enclosed with his very first letter to me.

He was reading poetry at a peace rally with several other actors. (I think that explains the doves in the foreground, though not necessarily the cage.)

But I digress.

Six weeks, and many letters and photos later, I flew to London over Thanksgiving, 1982. Roger's play had opened and was a big hit. Roger picked me up at Heathrow when I arrived early Saturday morning and drove me home. "Driving me home" didn't mean to Roger's house—he'd only just bought it and it was not yet habitable. There was scaffolding everywhere, and electricity and plumbing flowed to just one part of the house. Here's proof of scaffolding:

Rog and me prepping the front of his house for painting, 1982

His mum, however, lived next door. That's where Rog dropped me. On Lucy's doorstep. He introduced us, gave me a ticket for his play for that evening, and drove off to do the matinee. It was up to me and Lucy to get to know each other. So we did the proper English thing, and had tea.

Lucy was great. If she thought I was strange, she never let on. Well, maybe just a bit at the

Lucy Rees with Giffard, 1988

beginning. She put it right out there, asked me who the heck I was, how long I was planning to stay, how I felt about her son. Every time I showed up in London for the next seven years (and that's way more than a hundred times), the first thing she'd ask me was how long I was planning to stay. Very early on, she stopped asking how I felt about her son. The answer was obvious.

Just wed: Lucy and Bill

Lucy was born in 1910, had married Bill—a Lavender Hill policeman—and had two sons, Roger and, three years later, Andy. Bill died when Rog was a teenager, which required that Roger drop out of art school to support his mother and his brother. Eventually, he became an actor, and by the mid-1960s, after one failed attempt, he was accepted into the Royal Shakespeare Company.

Lucy was Roger's biggest fan, in a way that only a mum can be. Everyone at the RSC loved Lucy. And no one was prouder of Rog than his mum. When she figured out, which she did pretty quickly, that I was proud of Rog too, that I loved Rog deeply, and that he felt the same way about me, she accepted me as her third son without a second thought. I was part of the family. Proud to be so, too. Because I still wasn't out to my own family back in New York.

Roger and Lucy were great together. All his theatrical flair came from her. They were great friends and always had been.

On Thanksgiving 1984—two years after my first trip to London—Roger, Lucy, his brother, Andy, and Andy's wife, Carol, all came to New York to join my family for the holiday. Both families, under the same roof for the first time. My Grandma Mollie and Lucy were the same age, born the same year. They became girlfriends in two minutes flat. I wish I could find that picture!!

There were times I'd be in England on business when Roger was somewhere else, acting in a film or a television show, but I'd always go to South London to see Lucy,

Lucy and Roger in 1957 in London's Hyde Park

Here's Lucy with Roger's brother, Andy, and Nancy Coyne's daughter, Katie, when we stopped at Lucy's house for early dinner one afternoon in 1989.

take her for a meal, or better yet, sit down to some of her homemade wonders. We had become one big happy family. Or so I wanted to believe. That's when I decided to have "the talk" with my mom.

⊸⊰⊱ ⊰⊱⊶

When I first told my mother, Roz, the truth about me and Roger, she had a more difficult time than Lucy. My parents had already met Roger (who had become a regular fixture since that first Thanksgiving). He'd driven my folks all over town when they took a trip to London. My brother even celebrated his thirtieth birthday in Roger's dressing room in the West End—where the big surprise was a birthday cake, and *me!*

Left to right: my brother, Michael; Roger; Ruth Warrick (from Citizen Kane!*); me; and my sister-in-law, JoAnn, backstage at* The Real Thing *in London, January 1983*

My plan was (a) that everyone would love Rog so much, it wouldn't matter when (b) I explained to my folks that my love for Rog ran deeper than friendship.

Part A, check. Everybody loved Rog. So far, so good.

Part B—not so much. My mom had a hard time with the news.

My mom wanted all the things for me that she wanted for my

brother. A wife, a family, a life with an upward trajectory, grandchildren—everything she was raised to expect as normal. Everything *I* was raised to expect as normal. But, because Rog was at the center of my inability to fulfill my mom's wish list, he was not immediately greeted with unrestrained enthusiasm. We didn't talk about it much. That became our silent bargain, my mother and me. Silence.

Then, in 1989, Roger's brother, Andy, died very suddenly in May, and Lucy, heartbroken, passed away on Christmas Eve that same year. In the blink of an eye, Roger—grief-stricken—found himself without a family. He had a million friends, of course. No one's ever met Rog without loving him. And he had me. But he deserved more from me than silence. He deserved a family.

My mother, Roz, newly engaged to my father, Harold. They married in 1950.

So I went back to mine, and explained that *we* had to be Roger's family now. For my mom, I reserved this thought: *You now have an amazing opportunity. You can love this person who loves me more than I have any right to expect, and whom I love with all my heart. You can give us your acceptance and respect. And if you do, you'll reap the enormous reward of having this wonderful man always in your life.*

And she got it. She evolved, as they say. And in that wonderful way that mothers have, she became Roger's fiercest fan.

My brother became Roger's brother. My sister-in-law became Roger's sister. More about them, Michael and JoAnn: Rog and I depended on them for almost everything this past year—they're the rocks in our lives, and they've been so strong and smart and tireless and present for us, endlessly, selflessly so. There are no words, there is only awe, humility, and gratitude.

Fun times with Michael and Jo

Great Neck,
New York, 1991

New York, October 2014

New York,
November 2014

SIDEBAR: Michael and Jo stood with us as our witnesses on August 26, 2011, when Roger and I were married. Couldn't have done it without them.

RICK and ROGER
&
Engaged for 29 years.
Married in New York August 26, 2011

Oh, and – HAPPY HOLIDAYS!

Roger became uncle to my niece, Jenny, when she was two years old, and twenty-six years later, to her husband, Eric.

With Jenny and Eric Gatz/New York, Thanksgiving 2008

Roger became uncle to my nephew, Jeremy, when he was five years old, and a bit more recently to his wife, Nicole.

With Jeremy and Nicole Elice / A Hawaiian wedding, August 2009

Roger's crazy about Jenny and Eric's daughter, Mollie, seen below, celebrating her mommy's first Mother's Day!

Brooklyn, May 2012

And Rog adores Jeremy and Nicole's daughter, Vivienne (born January 7, 2014).

Los Angeles, May 2014

Harold, my amazing dad, has loved Roger like a son from the moment he knew that Roger loved his son—me—truly, deeply, wholeheartedly. Yay, Dad!! You're my hero—for a million reasons, and for this single one: loving Rog with your full heart.

Roger and me flanking my parents on a holiday cruise, 1994

From the same cruise: my Grandma Mollie and Grandpa Izzy were celebrating sixty-five years of marriage.

Over the years, we've been a perfectly imperfect, completely normal family. Just like I hoped we could be all those years ago, at our first Thanksgiving together in 1984.

Florida, January 2013

And just weeks before my parents celebrated sixty-five years of marriage themselves (in January of 2015), we all got together last Thanksgiving. The whole happy bunch of us. The family Roger married into, and has been a part of for decades. Here we are:

New York, November 28, 2014

But of all these friends and relatives, there is no one I'm prouder of, when it comes to Rog, than my mom. She came a long way, and it wasn't the easiest road for her, or for Rog. He just loved her, and kept on loving her, and pretty soon, she was loving him back. And they loved each other for years and years and years. Love works like that.

Rog, Roz, and me at my niece's wedding, September 2008

She chose not to live the "coulda-shoulda" life and show up to Roger's funeral with a heavy bag of regrets. Instead, she gave me and Rog the wonderful, blessed gift of an open heart. And what a reward she got in return. She made a friend for life. A friend who would plant her terrace for her . . .

. . . and slip in a couple of stones for her to find later. One that says "Awesome"—for that is what she has been to Rog—and another one that says "Joy"—for that is what she gives me by treating Rog like family.

Rog was a friend who appreciated the way she loves her sons, Michael and me . . .

. . . because that always reminded Rog of Lucy's love for him and Andy.

Rog was a friend who became a son himself, and spent his life happily in love with—and happy to be loved by—her baby, me.

Me and Rog, New Year's Eve 2014

So first—here's to you, Lucy. I think you must be hugging Rog right now up in heaven, and giving him a thick slice of ginger cake. I'm jealous, but I'm glad you have him back.

And to my extraordinary mother, who chose to give Roger Rees and Rick Elice the gift of acceptance, respect, and love. Thanks, Ma. This one's for you.

Lots of love to everyone,
Rick

THE THREE SISTERS RETURN

YESTERDAY, A PACKAGE ARRIVED in the mail from Edward Petherbridge, the thrilling actor/writer who was just here at 59E59 Theaters last month in his autobiographical hit, *My Perfect Mind*.

Paul Hunter and Edward Petherbridge, 2015

Edward visited Rog a lot in June when Rog was in the hospital with pneumonia. He's back in England now, and in the package he sent me was a DVD of the RSC production of Chekhov's *Three Sisters*. (I say Chekhov's, like there are all these other *Three Sisters* floating around.)

This *Three Sisters*—directed by Trevor Nunn—was part of the RSC's "Small Scale Tour" from July 1978 through April 1979. Also for the tour, Trevor (and John Amiel) directed Shakespeare's *Twelfth Night*—I say Shakespeare's, like there are all these other . . . oh, never mind. I'm a jerk.

Roger and Ian McKellan in 1978, during the RSC Small Scale Tour.

Trevor Nunn, left, directing The Three Sisters *in Stratford, 1978*

The tour also included an anthology show of literary gems, *Is There Honey Still for Tea*—inspired by the Rupert Brooke poem "The Old Vicarage" and created by Roger Rees, already in 1978 a hyphenate: artist-actor-writer.

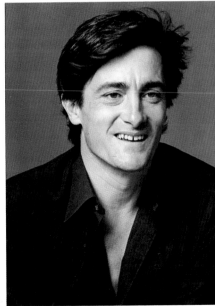

Rupert Brooke, 1887–1915   *Roger Rees, the young hyphenate, 1980*

The Small Scale Tour productions were mounted in Stratford and then traveled around the north of England on a shoestring budget and spit. A cloth backdrop, a couple of chairs, a few props, a truck with some costumes and lights—and off they went, this clutch of wonderful actors, to theaters, church halls, school gymnasia, bringing theater to the people.

Twelfth Night: *Ian McKellen, as Toby Belch, Roger as Sir Andrew Aguecheek, and Emily Richard as Viola, backstage in a gym near Newcastle, England, 1979*

For some additional context: Trevor Nunn's production of *Three Sisters* became life-sustaining to me in 1981 (through 1983).

Trevor Nunn and Roger, having completed the Small Scale Tour, 1979

On December 5, 1981—having spent eight and a half hours with the RSC and Roger . . . I staggered home to my little one-room studio on Fifty-Seventh Street and, just at midnight, flipped on the television at

Roger (Nicholas) and David Threlfall (Smike) in Nicholas Nickleby *during its original Broadway run, 1981*

the very moment that CBS Cable (a fledgling channel which eventually became A&E) began showing the RSC's production of Chekhov's *Three Sisters*. With all the same actors I'd just spent the day with at *Nickleby*!

Edward Petherbridge, who was so perfect as Newman Noggs, plays Vershinin. Emily Richard (Edward's wife), who played Kate Nickleby, is Irina. Suzanne Bertish, who played Fanny Squeers, is Masha. Janet Dale, Miss Nag the milliner, is Olga. Griffith Jones (Tim Linkinwater in NN) is Chebutiken; Bob Peck (John Brodie in NN) is Solyony. Patrick Godfrey, Mr. Kenwigs

Roger as Tusenbach / Three Sisters, 1978

in NN, is Masha's schoolteacher husband, Kulygin. Teddy Kempner and Rod Horn are there. (Tim Spall and Susan Tracy, as Andrei and Natasha, were not in NN.)

Oh, and Roger Rees, who had just struck me like lightning as Nicholas Nickleby, is Tusenbach, the doomed baron hopelessly in love with Irina.

SIDEBAR:

I'm a Yale Drama School graduate and a descendant of Russians. In 1981, I had a Chekhovian chip on my smart-ass shoulder the size of the troika dragged on by serfs in Andrei Serban's production of *Cherry Orchard* with Irene Worth and, among others, Meryl Streep. I didn't think the British could do Chekhov. I *knew* the British couldn't do it. What could be further from being Russian than being British? (Photographs of King George V and Czar Nicholas II notwithstanding.) In short, I was a snooty Chekhov snob, not about to change my mind about anything.

But in the flush of first infatuation, I had to watch this production. And I did, until about 3 a.m. I also taped it while I watched it. So I watched it over and over and over. I had friends over from Yale Drama School to watch it. I practically gave seminars on it. It was magnificent, it was perfection, it was ineffably sad, it was screamingly funny, it was utterly *Russian*! It was *the answer*! I had all the militant enthusiasm of the convert—the Brits *can* do Chekhov. They can be more Russian than my Russian grandparents! The British can do *anything*!! (And don't you think Roger is amazing as Tusenbach?)

The question with which I snagged Roger at our first meeting, a year later in September 1982, outside the Winter Garden Theatre stage door after a rehearsal of *Cats*—that moment where I thought, *Don't blow it, ask the right thing so he'll stay and talk to you,* was a deep, thoughtful, trenchant *Three Sisters* question. And it worked; Rog was intrigued, and we began, at that moment, a conversation about Chekhov, acting, theater, words, thoughts, actions, art, and life that lasted thirty-three years.

The following spring, in April of 1983, the RSC production of *All's Well That Ends Well*, also directed by Trevor Nunn (do we detect a pattern here?), arrived on the heels of *Cats* and wings of rave reviews in London, and settled into the Martin Beck (now Hirschfeld) Theatre. It was a wonderful production, presented by Liz McCann, Nelle Nugent, and the Shubert Organization. There was just one little hitch: we couldn't sell tickets. The cast members handed out fliers to

theatergoers on the TKTS line. The theatergoers were unmoved. But it was the RSC, and by 1983 I was in love with Roger and everything he ever touched or ever touched him. Which included the RSC. And anything, anyone to do with the RSC. How could I properly demonstrate my fealty to their enterprise, to these wonderful actors provisionally in New York City?

Roger was in the West End, starring in *The Real Thing*—

Roger and Felicity Kendal in the midst of the famous Cricket Bat Speech from Tom Stoppard's The Real Thing, *London 1982*

and was just about to sign off on going to France to make a film of the John Fowles novel *The Ebony Tower* with Laurence Olivier, Greta Scacchi, and Toyah Willcox.

I was on my own. So I did what any obsessive-compulsive theater nut would do—I invited the RSC to my one-room flat on Fifty-Seventh Street for a screening of *Three Sisters*, starring their RSC mates.

I offered them a Sunday afternoon of Chekhov and blini and caviar and vodka and glasses of tea from a samovar (I may be exaggerating slightly about the samovar) —just to "get their bottle back" as the saying goes. Me and twenty-five Brits crammed into my sorry little studio, getting loaded, watching Chekhov, telling stories, making toasts; blinis and bliss.

And then the RSC decamped for England. Once more, it was just me and my VHS.

Well, the VHS tape wore out long ago, and the VHS player is in the scrap heap of history. I figured I'd never see *Three Sisters*—this *Three Sisters*—again. Roger and I would go miles for any *Three Sisters* over the years. And we saw great productions and not-so-great productions—productions in English, productions in Russian, lavish productions, pared-down productions, starry productions, student productions. We even watch *Hannah and Her Sisters* three times a year because it has the word "sisters" in the title (and one of the greatest last lines ever: "Mickey, I'm pregnant." Gets me every time. But I digress.) Roger's *Three Sisters* though (the RSC "Small Scale"

production), I'd resigned myself to never see again. After the Small Scale Tour, Trevor rewarded Rog

Roger as Posthumus and Judi Dench as Imogen in Cymbeline *in Stratford, 1979*

with his first leading roles: Posthumus Leonatus in *Cymbeline*, directed by David Jones . . . and Semyon in Nikolai Erdman's *The Suicide*, directed by Ron Daniels.

Great quote about Rog in *The Suicide:* "Roger Rees's Semyon is funny, pitiable, admirable, and despicable in a performance of real intelligence, exactness, and precise observation. One of the very best performances I have seen in a long time."

(*Plays and Players*, July 1979;
review by Sally Eire)

After *The Suicide* came the experience that changed Roger's life . . .

All this came flooding back to me yesterday, when the envelope from Edward Petherbridge arrived containing the RSC "Small Tour" production of Chekhov's *Three Sisters*, directed by Trevor Nunn.

I watched it, for old time's sake, from midnight until about 3 a.m. To see Rog in it, to see them all, was like coming home.

The London poster for
The Life and Adventures of
Nicholas Nickleby, *1980*

Edward Petherbridge
(Vershinin) and Roger
(Tusenbach), as watched
last night by me

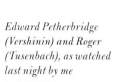

I know it so well, yet I missed it so much. A bit like the way Olga remembers Moscow. (That's Janet Dale as Olga in the bottom right of the preceeding photo.)

I felt like I became one with them, these British actors, these Russian characters, in this majestic comedy of missing something so much and not being able to do anything about it. In my case, what I miss so much is Rog. And there he is, on-screen, younger even than he was when he won the Olivier Award for *Nicholas Nickleby* in 1980 (below).

My beautiful, brilliant boy. So nice to see you again. Thank you, Edward.

Lots of love to everyone,
Rick

FINTY WILLIAMS /
A Speech at Roger's Memorial, New Amsterdam Theatre, September 21, 2015

I'm here on behalf of my mother, Dame Judi Dench, who is rehearsing in London. She so wanted to be here because she loved Roger. My parents met and worked with Rog for years at the Royal Shakespeare Company, and they loved Rog with the most extremely fierce love.

I loved him, too, like everybody else. But to go one step further, I actually asked Rog to marry me when I was four. Luckily for Roger, he met Rick, and we all loved him, too.

When I told my mother that the lights on Broadway had been dimmed in Roger's honor, she said, "Well, I doubt that when they come back on that they will ever burn as brightly again."

We have a favorite poem, my mother and I, written by the Kenyan poet and actor Kofi Awoonor. We think Rog might've liked it and we wanted to share it with you.

Weep not now, my love.
For as all die, so shall we.
But it is not the dying that should pain us.
It is the waiting, the intermission when we cannot act,
When our will is shackled by tyranny.
That hurts.
Yet somehow, I know the miracle of the world will be
wrought again.
The space will be filled in spite of the hurt,
By the immensity of love that will defy dying, and death.
Good night, my love.

God Bless, Roger.

EVEN AS A TREE

FIRST OF ALL, CORRECTIONS:
The other day I was listing Roger's big roles at the RSC that were his run-up to *Nicholas Nickleby.*

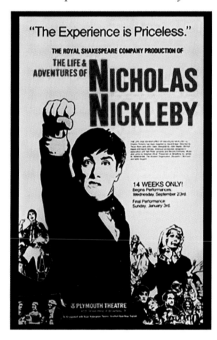

The Broadway poster for Nick Nick, 1981

I mentioned *Cymbeline* . . .

Ben Kingsley as Iachimo and Roger as Posthumus in Cymbeline

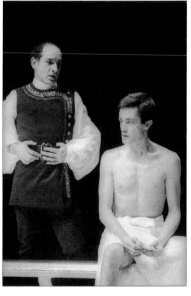

and I mentioned *The Suicide . . .* but I forgot all about *Comedy of Errors.* You RSC fans will remember this was the musical comedy version of the play, directed by Trevor Nunn, with songs by Trevor and Guy Woolfenden. Critics loved the originality of the production, and the polished slapstick and circus skills of the strong cast, which included Roger, Judi Dench, Richard Griffiths, Nickolas Grace, Michael Williams, Mike Gwilym, and Francesca Annis. It won the Olivier Award for Best New Musical in 1977.

Now go directly to YouTube, where you can watch parts of the production of *Comedy of Errors.* And Roger, with a perm.

You're welcome!

*Roger as Antipholus of Syracuse and Nickolas Grace as
Dromio of Ephesus*

*Left to right:
Francesca
Annis, Roger,
Richard
Griffiths as
The Officer,
Mike Gwilym
as Antipholus
of Ephesus,
and Judi
Dench*

AND NOW, TODAY'S REPORT.

Nancy Coyne told me to write this one.

Let me set the scene for you: I was watching Ted Petherbridge's DVD of *Three Sisters* the other night (as I may have told you), in which Roger plays Tusenbach, the doomed baron.

In Act 4, the final act, Tusenbach is one day away from achieving his great dream; he will marry Irina, and they will work and grow old together. It may not be a perfect marriage, she may not even return his love, but she respects and admires the Baron, and at last, at long, long last, she has agreed to marry him.

What Irina doesn't know is that the Baron's rival, Solyony, has challenged him to a duel. Tusenbach is about to leave to fight this duel. He's distracted. It doesn't seem like it will end well for him (and—spoiler alert! —it doesn't). Nevertheless, he goes off to fight.

Before he does, he takes his leave of Irina, and looks around at the woods that surround her house. And because the character is looking around, Roger happens to be looking right toward the camera as he delivers Tusenbach's last speech. And because he's looking toward the camera, it seemed to me—his chap—that he was looking directly at me.

And here's what Roger, looking directly at me, said the other night:

"I feel marvelous. It's as if I'm looking at these firs and maples and birch trees for the first time in my life. And they're looking back at me curiously and waiting. What beautiful trees. How beautiful life ought to be with them near. Look—there's a dead tree. Yet it still sways in the wind with the others. In the same way, I feel that were I to die, I should still take part in life in some way or other. Even as a tree."

It was so moving to me, looking at Roger looking at me, listening to him talking to me—well, kind of, since he was playing a character in a television

Rog with Nancy Coyne and Steve Karmen in 1993

Roger, at one with a tree, on Wandsworth Common in London, Christmas 1985

version of a play that was performed three years before we even met—but in the privacy of my own grief and the wee small hour of the morning when it happened, I started to cry. And I rewound it over and over, so he would turn toward me and look at me and speak to me over and over. And then, since it was 3 a.m., I pulled myself together, threw out the empty container of ice cream, and slipped into bed.

Me and Rog in Kyoto, 1984

When I woke up, it struck me that two days before he died, we planted a tree on the terrace where a Japanese maple had lived, planted in honor of a trip we'd made years ago to Japan. The poor maple didn't survive the brutal winter of 2014. So in May 2015, Roger dug it out and selected a new tree to be planted in its place.

The new tree, a Cascade snow cherry, was planted two days before Roger died. He was unable to plant it himself, but he watched, smiling, as two men planted it for us on Wednesday, July 8, 2015.

I mentioned this to Nancy and she said, "Well, that tree is Roger. You keep saying you can't find Roger—you just found him. The tree is Roger."

Now maybe it is or maybe it isn't. This morning when I watered it, I decided it is. But the fact is, Roger's attraction to trees . . .

The new Cascade snow cherry on our terrace, July 31, 2015

Roger, with older trees, in Williamstown / summer 2014

and his passion for nature
and gardens and growing things
in general . . . go way beyond his
performance as Tusenbach.
So I thought I'd take this opportunity to share some of those with you.

Roger in New York's Central Park, spring 2009

Roger in Ross-on-Wye, a beautiful river valley in Herefordshire, 1947

After Rog left *The Real Thing* and before he started filming *The Ebony Tower*, he drove us up to the Lake District for a few days. When I was a kid, my parents would take me and my brother up to Lake George in upstate New York at the end of the summer. We usually stayed at the same motel (The Georgian) and did the same

Lucy Rees, Granny Mabel Rees, Andy Rees, and Roger at the seaside in Bournemouth, 1951

things (boating, waterskiing, swimming during the day; miniature golf and eating in the evening). When I was an undergrad at Cornell, the campus was "high above Cayuga's waters," meaning Lake Cayuga, the longest of the Finger Lakes in that pristine region of upstate New York.

Me, photographed by Rog, at Lake Ullswater in the Lake region of England, summer 1983

Lake Ullswater was like Lakes George and Cayuga, only much less populated, and with so much more natural landscape and lake-scape. We stayed at Sharrow Bay, a bed-and-breakfast with an excellent restaurant. We weren't allowed to stay in the same room, being two men. Roger's room was called "Simplicity." Mine was "Phoebe." The first day, we hiked one way along the lake; the next day the other way. Being a city kid, I generally get antsy in the country (literally, as all insects seem irresistibly drawn to bite the heck out of me. But I digress . . .). Being with Rog, at the top of a fell or wading across an icy river, broke down my resistance to the natural world (well, kind of). Mostly, I loved what I saw and touched and smelled and walked through, because Roger loved it so much and seemed to understand it so well. He was my nature guide.

⁘⁘⁘ ———— ⁘⁘⁘

Early in 1984, before heading off to Stratford to begin rehearsals for *Hamlet*, Rog and I spent three days in Longboat Key, off the Gulf Coast of Florida by Tampa. His dear friend, Douglas Gordon, had a

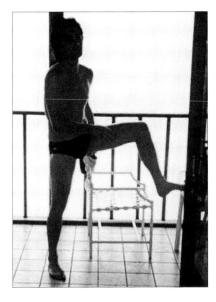

Roger at Douglas Gordon's oceanfront condo in Longboat Key, Florida, January 1984

place there that was right on the water.

Every day, we'd sit on the sand and run lines. Then we'd go into the sea. Then we'd walk along the beach, have a sandwich, rinse, and repeat. From Tampa, we drove across the state to Orlando to spend a day at Walt Disney World. It was there that Roger first saw how a pineapple grows.

Roger, with pineapple, at Walt Disney World in Orlando, January 1984

Castles were something Roger had already seen in England. But this one wasn't in ruins.

We pretended the Cinderella Castle at the park was Kronborg Castle in Denmark (called Elsinore in *Hamlet*)—although the Elsinore in the photo below looks very different. The Castle in Denmark was the seat of power in *Hamlet*. Now we sat on the battlement at Walt Disney World, running lines from Shakespeare's greatest play. This was likely the only time *Hamlet* played at the Cinderella Castle.

Roger at Disney World's Cinderella Castle, January 1984. And at Elsinore, June 1984

Later, when it came time for us to get some permanent digs in New York, Roger liked one particular building because it reminded him of a castle. Maybe a bit more like the Alhambra in Spain than the Cinderella Castle in Orlando. But a castle nonetheless. Surrounded by Roger's favorites: green things of all shapes and sizes that grow in the sun.

The wonderful thing about having a park on two sides of our castle is this: on the Hayden Planetarium side, we have fountains. On

the Central Park side, we have proper lakes. It's not Cayuga or Ullswater, but it's pretty gorgeous, and, while entirely man-made, it offers the illusion of a stunning natural environment. So it's everything Roger adored: a great effect, thanks to a brilliant design—comprised only of elements occurring in nature. I always got the feeling that both parks adored Roger as much as he loved them.

Our very own castle: The Beresford apartments (top, bottom) in New York City

When Roger was playing in *Hamlet* and *Love's Labour's Lost* at Stratford, he had a week off when a new show was being put into the repertory. So off we went in his Morris Ital (the make of his car),

Roger at Tintern Abbey in Wales, summer 1984

driving through Herefordshire, to see where his Granny Mabel was buried, where she lived, and where she worked. Up to Malvern, where we drank bottles and bottles of local sparkling water, then west into Wales, where we stopped at Tintern Abbey to touch those fabled ruins with our own hands.

On the way down to London, Roger took me to Avebury, to see the ring of stones. It's not as famous a site as Stonehenge, but neither is it as crowded. We marveled at the circle of giant stones, then noticed it was getting dark. We hopped back into the Morris Ital and headed down a road that seemed like it was paved. Pretty soon, we realized it wasn't. Then, CRACK!! And the car slowed down and stopped. We looked behind us to see what we'd hit. It was a rock in the unpaved road that sheared the gearbox of the Morris Ital right off. As we got out of the car, night fell. We were in a field, on a dirt road, with a dead Morris Ital and a severed gearbox. And it was very dark. And it was fifteen years before cell phones. In the distance, we saw what looked like a light in what looked like a farmhouse. So we tramped across the corn for about twenty minutes, walked up to the front door of the house, and knocked. The woman inside let Roger in to call for a tow truck. I stood outside because she, very sensibly, declined to allow two strangers into her home.

Then we headed back across the field to find the car. About three hours later, a pair of headlights came bouncing towards us. A tow truck arrived like our very own deus ex machina, to give us a tow to Swindon, the nearest place where there was a garage. It being about 4 a.m. when the tow truck dropped us there, the garage was closed. So we left a note on the windshield, left the car, and walked a few roads over to a Trusthouse Motel. We took a room, then headed up to bed. About five minutes later, there was a knock on the door. "Are there two men in this room?" Against Trusthouse Motel policy, apparently. Since Roger was already sound asleep, I left a note on the mirror and moved to another room. Ah, Swindon.

The next morning we got someone to look at the car. A Morris Ital gearbox was sent for, and Roger took me by bus to neighboring Cheltenham for lunch. This prolonged visit in the west counties of England was beautiful, and since then, I've been a sucker for the elegant Cheltenham serif font on my computer. If the Trusthouse Motel in Swindon had a font, I'm sure it would be sans serif, sans hospitality, and sans my business.

Thirty years later, Rog was back at Tintern Abbey.

Rog on his last trip to England, September 2014

Chuzenji is the small lakeside town where the natives go to get away from tourists crowding into Tokyo. Roger's friend, Yoji Aoi, took R&R to Chuzenji for some R&R—hot springs to bathe in, beautiful forests to wander through, and a long, placid lake to boat on.

It was in Chuzenji that a tiny, wizened Japanese masseuse threw me on a tatami mat, laid her tiny, wizened hands on my back, and asked Yoji how long I'd been having stomach problems. How she knew that I'd been suffering from diverticulitis during the trip, I'll never know. But an hour later, for the first time in a week, I had relief from the pain. I've been a firm believer in shiatsu massage as nature's medicine ever since.

Roger and me with students, enjoying the lakeside charms of Lake Chuzenji, Japan, in 1984

Rog at Canyon Ranch in Tucson, Arizona, 1987

Rog, a devoted gardener, spent hours reading about flowers, birds, trees—sketching them, photographing them, teaching me about them with such delight. He was instinctively connected to the natural world, and always at peace with it. His calm surety was hardy in him, hardy like the giant succulents dotting the American deserts. He loved driving through Death Valley, he loved hiking through Sedona, and he loved our yearly visits to Canyon Ranch. Later, at the house in Studio City, California, he created a sun garden, a shade garden, a wet garden, and a dry garden—and experimented, transplanted, pruned, and trained his trees and plants until he gained a real working knowledge of that climate so different from England's and conditions so much more challenging.

Marcus Stapleton Martin and Roger at Norbury in Derbyshire, 1987

Rog met Marcus Stapleton Martin at one of the readings of *Is There Honey Still for Tea?*—an anthology show he put together during the RSC Small Scale Tour in 1978. Marcus was a country squire who lived alone in a magnificent Queen Anne manor house next to a gem of a church (St. Mary and St. Barlok), part of which was a Norman chapel that was nine hundred years old. The whole place was called Norbury. The main house dated from the seventeenth century, but there was also part of a medieval stone house with a feasting hall with stained glass that was historically important. The stained glass in the church was also renowned. People would travel from all over to see it and photograph it. The Fitzherberts were lords of the manor for centuries—and Marcus, distantly related to the Fitzherberts, acquired it in 1963.

SIDEBAR:

For you fans of the Regency period, Mrs. Fitzherbert, a Catholic widow, secretly married the future King George IV in 1785, but the marriage was illegal since any marriage by a member of the royal family under twenty-five had to be approved by the king. Even worse, a royal heir marrying a Catholic was barred from succession. The couple stayed together until 1803 but had no children; Mrs. Fitzherbert was then given a pension of £5,000 a year, which was a lot of *dosh* in those days.

Behind the house was an herb garden that struck me like a miniature Versailles in its geometric exactitude, then a prospect down to the River Dove. The approach to the house was striking: a beech-tree allée leading up to the house that seemed at least the length of a football field (American football, that is), anchored at each side by a brick folly. It was quite a place.

When Rog brought me out to Marcus's pile for a weekend, the old boy took a shine to me. At our last breakfast together on the Monday, he made us an extraordinary proposal. He wanted to leave the two of us this house and these grounds. He was moved to have met us as a couple, and so pleased to see "two young people" who had found what had eluded him all his otherwise very privileged life: love and companionship. He thought it would be very nice indeed to have us carry the estate's torch for him after he shuffled off. "Think it over," he said. "It's a life's work, but I've enjoyed it. The place has got to be looked after by people who love it or it'll crumble away. Otherwise, it's going to the National Trust."

We drove back to Bristol, where Rog was in residence at the Bristol Old Vic as associate artistic director. We were tickled by the notion and we loved the gigantic, life-changing drama of Marcus's invitation. But it was too big an idea for us at the time; taking over the responsibility for a house like that, and grounds like that, was a full-time job, a big commitment. And we both already had full-time jobs and big commitments. So Marcus left his house to the National Trust, which has protected it and maintained the rooms of rare books, the windows of treasured glass, and the walls of the ancient stone chapel.

But Rog and I often wondered what our lives would've been like if we'd packed up and moved to Derbyshire, bought a couple of pairs of

Wellington boots, found ourselves a good old dog, and become country squires like Marcus. Marcus Stapleton Martin passed away shortly after our visit, and he is remembered, fondly, here.

In 1988, Rog was back in the West End, with Felicity Kendal and Nigel Hawthorne in Tom Stoppard's *Hapgood*. One Sunday, he said, "Let's drive out to the country. I need to see some trees. Oh, and we need to take our tuxes." Okay. And off we headed for East Sussex, which is, well, east of Sussex. After hiking through some

Roger and Felicity Kendal in Hapgood/ *London, 1988*

Rog near Lewes Castle, en route to Glyndebourne in East Sussex, 1988

pastures and climbing up to the barbican at Lewes Castle, we wiped ourselves off—it was pouring—and changed our clothes in the car. Roger had gotten us a couple of tickets to Verdi's *Falstaff* at Glyndebourne, where you have to wear evening clothes even though you're picnicking on the (soaking wet) ground. Roger was no longer drinking in 1988, but I had what was called a Pimm's Cup. It's the only thing I remember about Verdi's *Falstaff.*

Roger, Judy Davis, and Simon Jones in Los Angeles for Hapgood, *1989*

When *Hapgood* moved from London to Los Angeles, Roger went with it. Judy Davis replaced Felicity Kendal. Simon Jones replaced Nigel Hawthorne. Rog had always had a passion for Los Angeles. He loved the climate, and he loved what could be grown in that climate.

While he was playing in *Hapgood*, he auditioned for *Cheers*. When Rog was cast as a recurring character, Robin Colcord, he needed a place to live. In Studio City, we found a small house with a big garden, and Rog got to work. While I pulled out ivy for days on end, Rog planned terraces. We'd scour Mulholland Drive for construction sites, fill the car with stones and bricks, and bring 'em back to the garden. Little by little, what was large but unremarkable, was transformed by Rog the gardener into a four-terraced multi-climate garden with cacti, grapevines, fig, apricot, olive, and grapefruit trees, all bearing their fruit. We built pathways and fences and

The parody magazine cover that introduced Roger's character on Cheers.

arbors and pergolas and stairs. Roger's green thumb was prodigious; he literally threw a schefflera over the deck, and it rooted and grew to a height of about forty feet! Rog was never happier. Every now and then he went to Paramount and hung out with the *Cheers* gang. But mostly what he did was work in the garden. And whenever I was there, I mostly worked in the garden, too.

Looking down from the sun garden toward the dry garden at the bottom of the dell in 1991

Looking up to the sun garden and the house, 1992

Roger (third from left) taking a break from the garden with some white-water rafting. I was not in the raft on this 1993 trip because, well, somebody had to take the photo.

Good times, good garden. The last thing we did when we sold the house in 2005 was plant a baby palm tree on the far side of the lowest terrace. Now when we drive past the house, that palm towers over the property, a new landmark. Rog loved that.

∽✥ ⸺ ✥∽

Speaking of palm trees, Rog loved them, too. His brother, Andy, worked at British Airways. Between Roger's RSC tours and Andy's family discount, there was nowhere on earth that Roger hadn't visited before I met him. But in 1994, I conspired with his manager, Alan Siegel, to clear a week for a surprise trip to Maui to celebrate Roger's fiftieth birthday. As soon as I purchased the nonrefundable tickets, Roger picked up four days' work on an episode of *My So-Called Life* and our Hawaiian week shrank to three days. All we did was sit under the palms. Roger loved the trees. I loved that the palms were very close to the all-you-can-eat buffet.

Roger celebrating his fiftieth birthday in Maui, 1994

In 2001, Roger got to play founding father John Adams in Peter Stone's great musical *1776*, as part of the LA Reprise season that year. It just so happened that they were performing the show in September. When 9/11 occurred, Rog led a concert to raise money for the Ground Zero effort, and the next night, the company returned to performing *1776*. Peter Stone, who'd always been a fan of Roger's, came out west to see it and was very pleased.

When Rog came back east, we were invited to visit Peter and Mary Stone on Long Island. Outside their door, there was a huge field of wildflowers that Roger found absolutely enchanting.

Roger in Peter Stone's wildflower field in Long Island, 2002

New York Theatre Workshop production of Peter and the Starcatcher, *2011*

In 2011, Roger and Alex Timbers directed *Peter and the Starcatcher* at New York Theatre Workshop in the East Village. There isn't a lot of grass or plants or trees in the East Village. But inside the theater on East Fourth Street, Roger and Alex created—out of pieces of plastic, a few sticks, some umbrellas, and a length of rope—an island jungle so thick with trees and undergrowth that you couldn't tell whether it was day or night.

When we were rehearsing *Peter and the Starcatcher* at New York Theatre Workshop, someone had organized a small cactus garden in their kitchen/greenroom area. Roger liked that sill full of cacti, and began his own collection on our bathroom windowsill.

Part of Roger's bathroom cactus collection, which he started in 2011

In the summer of 2013, my brother and sister-in-law, Michael and JoAnn; plus their kids, Jeremy and Nicole (very pregnant); and Jennifer and Eric, with Mollie (then two and a half), organized a family trip to Napa Valley. Rog and I were in Denver for the opening of the first national tour of *Peter and the Starcatcher,* and we headed west to join them. Roger was growing his mustache for the Broadway production of *The Winslow Boy.*

Rog among the grapes in Wine Country, August 2013

Last summer, we were lucky enough to get to work together again on a little musical I wrote with Michael Patrick Walker called *Dog and Pony.* Roger directed the world premiere production at The Old Globe in San Diego. We were assigned digs that overlooked Petco Park, where the Padres play. A longtime baseball fan, I couldn't have been happier to live next door to the stadium. From our terrace, I could catch the final innings whenever there was a home game.

*Me behind Petco Park's outfield in
San Diego, June 2014*

Roger never cared much for baseball; he couldn't grasp the concept. He did, however, love to hug the palm trees that lined the entrance—mere steps from where we lived while working on the show.

*Roger and the palms of San Diego,
where the Padres play, June 2014*

Last fall, a tree on the Great Lawn in Central Park turned such a bright red. Roger had already had his first brain surgery and was feeling really well as we walked through the park to begin his first round of radiation therapy . . .

Roger in Central Park, November 2014

Roger at the Rockefeller Center Christmas Tree, December 23, 2014

and when we were getting ready to drive up to see our friends, Tom Schumacher and Matthew White, for Christmas, Roger said, "I want to see the tree at Rockefeller Center before we go." It was a very tall tree that year.

In February, we took our last trip together. I was set to participate in a group sales event for *Jersey Boys* in advance of our run of the show in Dublin. It was just before Roger was due to begin rehearsals for *The Visit* on Broadway. So we turned it into a little Valentine's Day vacation. A dozen years after Roger's beautiful performance as a bus conductor inspired by Oscar Wilde in *A Man of No Importance*, he got to meet Oscar face-to-face at the Wilde memorial in St. Stephen's Green—a beautiful park where the statue of Wilde is surrounded by trees.

Roger and Oscar Wilde in St. Stephen's Green in Dublin, Ireland, February 14, 2015

When we got home from Dublin, Central Park was covered in snow.

Rog and me in Central Park, February 18, 2015

To bring this Roger Report about trees to its conclusion, let me share with you two wonderful gifts from Steve and Judy Orich, and from Catherine Schreiber—all of whom realized, without ever seeing Roger's Tusenbach speech in *Three Sisters*, that a tree is the perfect way to honor Rog and to remember him.

Thank you, dear friends, for getting it so right.

Trees for Israel

ב' תבֹיאֵ אֵל הֹאֵרֵין וֹנֵטֵעֵתֵם (יקרא יט:כג)
"When you shall come to the land you shall plant trees." – Leviticus 19:23

A Circle Of Five Trees Will Be Planted
In Honor Of
Roger Rees
May This Serve As
A Living Tribute To His Memory
Steve & Judy Orich

JEWISH
NATIONAL
FUND
Your Voice in Israel

For mine is an old belief...
there is a soul in every leaf. M. M. Ballou

A grove of five trees
has been dedicated
to honor
the life of

Your Beloved Husband
Roger Rees

A contribution to TreePeople
has been made by

Catherine Schreiber
With all my love

This meaningful gift and the restoration it makes possible, is at the
heart of TreePeople's effort to encourage personal involvement in
restoring and caring for our natural environment.

TREEPEOPLE   421781

12601 Mulholland Drive
Beverly Hills, California 90210
Tree Dedications (818) 753-8733
www.treepeople.org

Printed with soy ink on 100% recycled paper.
Design by KK Design

This morning, August 1 (White Rabbits, Rog!), I can see the same carpet of trees from the terrace that Roger would see every day.

Central Park, August 1, 2015

I'll close with this image of my darling Rog, my tree-loving, seed-sowing, plant-saving nature boy. I will try to see him in every blade of grass and every leafy branch. I hope you will, too.

"I feel that were I to die, I should still take part in life in some way or other. Even as a tree."
—Tusenbach,
Three Sisters

Thank you, Nancy.
Lots of love to everyone,
Rick

NANCY COYNE /
A Speech at Roger's Memorial, New Amsterdam Theatre, September 21, 2015

I met Roger over thirty years ago in London. I'd known about him for a couple of years before that, not just as Nicholas Nickleby, but as the love interest of my best friend, Rick Elice. I watched in those early days as Rick flew to London *every weekend*, and I'm not exaggerating, so they could be together while Roger was performing in the West End in Tom Stoppard's *The Real Thing*. Rick and Roger were, in fact, the real thing. Rick was so devoted to Roger and made so many trips across the pond that British Airways actually sent him Christmas presents. And I'm not talking about pins and totes and blankets. I'm talking cashmere sweaters from Burberry, beautifully wrapped and hand-delivered.

So I was curious to meet the man who inspired all that mileage. And when I did, I understood immediately. Roger and I quickly discovered how much we had in common. We both loved theater. We both loved Rick. And we both loved wine.

In fact, we loved wine so much that Rick became sort of our personal sobriety coach. And Roger became part of my support group. He never failed to tell me one of his stories that always ended, "And there but for the grace of God and Rick go I." Like the New Year's Eve party they attended, when a particularly lubricated guest decided to leave but couldn't find his coat. Hardly able to stand, he demanded that the host— some actor fellow named Laurence Olivier—locate his missing Burberry immediately. Roger's hilarious reenactment of the drunk foreshadowed his brilliant Lord Marbury on *The West Wing*. But mostly, he said, he was always so grateful he would never have to be that person again.

Roger had three defining qualities: gratitude, responsibility, and a unique talent for loving. It was gratitude that distinguished Roger from the crowd. When given the choice to see what he lacked or rejoice in what he had, Roger never made the wrong choice. He was most grateful, of course, that he had found Rick, and Rick's family, to love.

Yes, when Roger loved you, he loved your family, too. The whole *mishpachah*—as he would say, after he converted to Judaism. One winter night years ago, when my parents were visiting from Washington, we all had dinner. They had tickets for *The Phantom of the Opera*, and Rick and Roger volunteered to walk them to the theater. Later, back at their hotel, they were all atwitter—and this was long before Twitter—and my mother explained that *Phantom* had not really been my father's cup of tea, but that Rick and Roger had been waiting in the snow outside the Majestic Theatre to walk them home. "*That* was our favorite part of the night," my mother said. Lily Tomlin said it even better: "The show was soup. The walk home with Roger was art."

It was also responsibility that set Roger apart. Responsibility that began with the audience. Roger, who never said an unkind word about anyone, made an exception for movie stars who skipped performances to do promotion for an upcoming film. He felt that the little old lady in the balcony was somebody's mother who had paid her hard-earned money to see that show, and all the actors, even the stars, owed it to her to show up.

You see, everyone Roger loved was some version of the mother he loved so well. In South London, on Wandsworth Common, was the tiny row house where Roger's mother, Lucy, lived.

When the house next door was for sale, of course Roger bought it so he could be close by. And so nobody would ever have to go outside to visit the other, he knocked down a wall between the two homes.

You think he put in a door? He did not. He built a secret bookcase that swung open to reveal a whole house on the other side. If Lucy needed Rog, she needed only to lean on the collected works of William Shakespeare, and Roger would be right there behind them. Roger's talent for loving never dimmed, even on his dying day. On my last visit to see him, he whispered to me one question: "Will Rick be okay?" And I assured him, as I suspect many of us did, that Rick would be okay and that we'd all see to it.

I have only one regret: Roger and I promised each other that, on his eightieth birthday, we would toast our mutual sobriety with very expensive champagne. But I'm consoled by the belief—a belief so strong that it almost passes for knowledge—that at 8 p.m. on July 10, 2015, the moment Roger left us, the role of Saint Peter was being played by that same Laurence Olivier who greeted Roger with a hug and two silver flutes. One, being played by an angel. The other, filled with God's own house champagne. I can hear Roger toasting us all.

"Cheers." One word that, whenever we hear it, we'll know that sweet, gentle Roger is near.

STARCATCHER OF WILLIAMSTOWN

THE OTHER DAY, I FOUND MYSELF standing on Sixth Avenue, looking up at a building. I was on recon for our attorney's office, where I was due yesterday to sign some more papers. There are lots of papers to sign when your spouse passes away.

The last time I was in that building was to sign papers *with* Rog. It was October 10, 2014, a Friday. We were there with our friend and business manager, Brandon Chapnick, and a group of attorneys. We signed and signed and signed. Then Roger went to a tap-dancing class (he was about to start rehearsals for *The Bandwagon* at City Center and wanted to impress Kathleen Marshall, the director, whom Rog adored). He got home at about 7 p.m., with flowers—just because. About two hours later, he had a splitting headache, which overpowered him. It was the first indication that something was seriously wrong. By Sunday afternoon, we were in the hospital.

So you can appreciate why I think of this building on Sixth Avenue with some trepidation. Having reminded myself exactly which was the cross street, I turned and continued south on my way to meet my pal Christian for lunch.

As I continued to walk, I realized the building across the street was the former New York headquarters of now-defunct British Caledonian Airways.

Once—and only once—I flew on British Caledonian.

~~~

Milton Goldman, a legendary ICM agent, and the American point man for all the Brit actors of note, represented Rog in the 1980s. He took a shine to me, and when he realized all the trips I was making to London to see Rog, he secured me a trip on British Caledonian. All I had to do was bring a case of wine on board with me, hand the wine to the crew, and I'd be given a complimentary first-class trip. During the flight, the crew would pour wine for the passengers and talk about the label, the vineyard, etc. All I had to do was enjoy my first-ever first-class passage to London.

It was 1986, December. Snow was falling. The first-class cabin was half empty, darkened for comfort. The stewardesses were completely sweet. There was no pressure. I sat in the wide seat, watching the snow fall, knowing that six hours away, Roger would be waiting for me at Gatwick, and I would see my love for thirty-six hours. I felt like I was in a very romantic theater story by Evelyn Waugh. It was an entirely happy moment in my life.

Roger didn't require first-class trappings to make him entirely happy. All he needed was to be near a theater. On our last trip together—to Dublin on Valentine's Day—Rog was very excited about visiting Smock Alley Theatre. It's the oldest extant theater in Ireland, from 1662, I think. Rog wanted to see it, partly because Smock Alley was where *The Recruiting Officer, The Beaux Strategem, The Rivals,* and *School for Scandal* were first performed—all of which Roger appeared in and/or directed. But mostly it is because it's where David Garrick, Roger's hero, the great eighteenth-century actor, first played Hamlet. Roger couldn't get enough of David Garrick. We have shelves of books about him.

Roger was ecstatic when we found Smock Alley Court and the theater facing the river. It's still a working theater; there's even a theater school adjoining the old building.

Standing in front of the theater, and behind, in the courtyard . . .

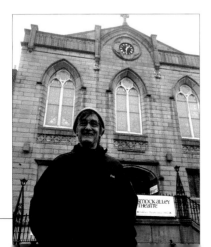

Roger feeds the birds outside Smock Alley Theatre, Dublin, Ireland, February 15, 2015.

was such a genuine thrill for Rog. All he needed was to be near a theater. It was an entirely happy moment in his life.

And then, as always, he put aside his pleasure to give comfort to God's little creatures—in this case, some Irish pigeons.

He'd been carrying that bag of bread and seeds all morning, just to feed the birds of Dublin. Here, on one knee, he is really and truly happy.

That was only February.

⁓⧽———⧼⁓

This morning, our friend Alex Timbers sent a link to a story about Roger and theater that tells you everything you need to know about why theater—the buildings, of course, but mostly the people who work in them—gave Rog such pleasure. I first met Alex in 2005. It was Roger's first summer as artistic director at Williamstown Theatre Festival—a job he adored for so many reasons.

Alex Timbers, me, and Rog, at rehearsals in 2013

David Garrick was Roger's hero. Roger was ours. Alex describes why on the following pages, in a tribute from *American Theatre* magazine.

Roger, who wore his status lightly

STARCATCHER OF WILLIAMSTOWN

The iconic actor was also a great artistic director, a tireless theater enthusiast, and a gracious mentor to young artists.

By Alex Timbers

I met Roger in June 2005, when I was a directing assistant at Williamstown Theatre Festival, during the first summer he ran the festival. All of the young apprentice actors and directors were completely in his thrall from moment one, myself included. Not only was this a legendary Olivier- and Tony Award-winning RSC actor existing among us plebeians, but, boy, was he an equally gifted director. To this day, his ingenious, elemental production of *Herringbone* at Williamstown, starring B. D. Wong, has to be among my top ten favorite nights at the theater.

Both those skills were secondary, however, to his brilliance as an artistic director. Williamstown is a unique place in that the directing assistant job entails not only programming a diverse, overlapping season of plays and musicals (which he did remarkably well for three seasons) but also involves a mentorship role to the many young actors and directors who make up the apprentice, non-Equity, and directing corps programs. And Roger relished his role as mentor at least as much as his more showy job as summer theater kingmaker.

To me, that was the defining feature of Roger: his dedication to and genuine respect for what he described as the "next generation" of American theater. While he was tirelessly tending to all the needs of a huge organization and an insane production schedule, he was a regular fixture at the eccentric one-evening-only midnight shows of all the young people working at the festival. How he had the time and energy to attend those and then be in rehearsal or donor breakfasts the next morning, day after day, I have no idea. But he cared deeply about these young actors, directors, writers, designers, and technicians, and it mattered to him that these lark-ish projects were happening; indeed, he viewed the people creating them as the lifeblood of the festival. There was no wall around Roger or hurdles to be able to talk to him. His unpretentious nature and genuine joy and enthusiasm for theater were infectious to us all.

At Williamstown, he created the Leapfrog program to unite early career directors, writers, and the non-Equity company of actors in the creation of original plays and musicals. He chose two projects a year, allowing each an unusually in-depth investigation and long rehearsal periods. He wanted the shows to arrive as merely ideas, without text, so that the cross-collaboration of actors, director, and writers could inform the creation of the shows and infuse them with as much energy and invention as possible.

I was lucky enough to be a part of that program my second year at Williamstown, and from it *Bloody Bloody Andrew Jackson* was born. Michael Friedman and I began the summer thinking the show was going to be a play with songs, and emerged with a full-blown musical, replete with dance, underscoring, the whole nine yards. I was a director at the start of the summer, but by the end, I was a book writer, too. A nonunion actor up there named Danny Mefford was recruited to do some movement, traveled to Broadway with the show, and is now one of the most prolific choreographers working today, with musicals like *Fun Home* and *Bridges of Madison County*. That lack of preciousness about titles and formal experience was central to how Roger viewed the world.

Roger was an actor, a writer, a director, a producer, and a painter. To him, there was no reason that a person had to be only one thing or the other, and that ethos informed the entire spirit of those lucky enough to be at his theater during those three magical years.

When I asked Roger the summer before if I could flip the orientation of the church where we did my show, *Dance Dance Revolution*, and cast the local head of police as the villain, he was all for it. A futuristic musical that used preexisting rave music for toddlers as its sound track wasn't the kind of show you would typically associate with the refined tradition of Williamstown—and that made Roger all the more excited about it.

In fact, while Roger's career is in some ways associated with canonical plays, he was an even greater lover and advocate for new work. He championed a second stage that only featured new plays and wouldn't allow them to be reviewed, so he could foster a protective environment. How cool is that?

Working on *Peter and the Starcatcher* united his love for new work and his dedication to younger actors. This show, which began for us as a workshop in a log cabin in his third year as artistic director, was a natural extension of those dual focuses. He was so excited about the fact that the play required a deft cast of fresh-out-of-school actors, which he would again routinely describe as the "next generation" of American theater.

And, indeed, there was nothing more inspiring than watching said actors receive notes from him. Not only were his thoughts always insightful and effective—and suffused with his characteristic charm and wit—but they were incredibly entertaining and filled with his passion for making theater.

This passion was at times eccentric, and Roger had a true childlike joy that made him a perfect match for Peter Pan. Despite his many film roles and being Nicholas Nickleby, he was not above joining in the Williamstown late-night cabaret

and singing a silly song in front of the festival staff

Alex Timbers and Roger at the Broadway opening of Peter and the Starcatcher

and patrons. Or dressing up head to toe as a full-on sea captain with me at the *Peter and the Starcatcher* opening night.

One of my favorite memories of Roger was when we were preparing to do *Peter* on Broadway and Roger wanted to take the cast on a field trip to an actual ship to get a sense of the scale of a real sailing vessel, and perhaps what it might be like to be aboard one in a storm: what the planks might feel like, what a mizzenmast really was. Also, it would be a hoot.

So he pushed for it. And, probably as surprisingly to him as to the rest of us, he got his wish.

Roger, right, leads a tour of the Peking, *a nineteenth-century ship in New York's South Street Seaport, with the cast of* Peter and the Starcatcher, *including David Rossmer, foreground.*

One day in February, the producers organized vans and the entire cast and design team went down to South Street Seaport; we boarded the *Peking* and walked around. We walked on the planks and looked at the mizzenmast, laughed and had a great time imagining the whole play, as it might have happened in real life.

That passion for the communal experience and for the group of young artists who might one day look after another "next generation" of actors and directors were what defined Roger Rees to me.

Thank you, Alex.
Lots of love to everyone,
Rick

DAVID GARRICK

FIRST, AN ADDENDUM: The other day, I mentioned Roger's affection for David Garrick, the great eighteenth-century English actor/manager. His first great role was Richard III, which propelled him to stardom and enabled him to manage the Theatre Royal, Drury Lane.

David Garrick as Richard III

Roger collects porcelain images of this scene. These figurines are early examples of theater merch. They were cast and sold to fans in the mid-1700s as mementos of Garrick's indelible performance.

Roger's collection of David Garrick merch

AND NOW, TODAY'S REPORT . . .

Yesterday, Edward Petherbridge forwarded me this photo of Emily Richard (his wife) as Kate and Roger as Nicholas, during the filming of *Nicholas Nickleby* for television in 1980.

Emily Richard (Kate) and Rog (Nicholas),
on the set of Nicholas Nickleby, *1980*

Seeing Rog in that particular coat made me remember something. I wrote about it to Edward, who thought it was interesting enough to post on his blog. Since Edward is never wrong, I thought I'd share it with you today.

Turns out, after the filming of the play for television, after the RSC had come to New York—which Manny Azenberg reminded me the other day only happened thanks to the historic partnering of the Nederlanders and the Shuberts, who teamed up to share the risk—and after *Nickleby* concluded its Broadway engagement and everything was packed up and returned to England, Roger kept the coat. He loved it,

he couldn't part with it, so
he kept the coat.

For years, it was hanging
in the closet.

Years later, Rog was
back on Broadway for the
Roundabout production of
Anouilh's *The Rehearsal*,
directed by the late, great
Nicky Martin. The cast
included Anna Gunn, Fred
Weller, David Threlfall
(Smike in *Nickleby*),
Frances Conroy, and
Roger.

Frances Conroy and Rog in The Rehearsal
at the Roundabout Theatre, 1996

During this time, Broadway
Cares/Equity Fights AIDS had
scheduled an event in Shubert
Alley that concluded with a charity
auction of Broadway memorabilia.

Roger decided to donate his
precious *Nicholas Nickleby* coat.
He was sad to see it go, but Rog
was part of the community and the
community needed the coat more
than he did.

Rog in The Rehearsal. *Thank you, Joan
Marcus, fabled theater photographer.*

Shubert Alley was mobbed with people. It was a Saturday afternoon between the matinees and evening performances, so clutches of actors mingled with legions of fans, and lots of amazing stuff was being auctioned off.

Eventually, Roger's Nickleby coat was shown. The bidding started slowly, but the pace picked up dramatically when someone from the back of the crowd began upping the bid. Finally, it sold for a rather healthy sum. Roger missed the moment, having not been able to get over from his theater in time.

But that night, when he came home, Rog received a call from the charity, telling him that the coat went for a lot of money. He was very pleased to have parted with his beloved coat for such a good cause.

I was pleased, too. Perhaps, Roger intuited, a little *too* pleased. "And what are you so happy about?" he asked me, rather pointedly. I shrugged. "Go look in the closet," I said.

He opened the door, and there was his coat, hanging in its usual spot. "I was the high bidder," I said. "This way, we can auction it off again next year."

Which is exactly what we did.

The Nickleby coat was one of Roger's favorite costumes. But I think the costume he loved most was not from any production of any play. It was Roger's "dream costume"—the one he picked to reveal his true personality—and he only wore it once, in 1984. It was for a photo session for *Red Shoes*, a coffee-table book by Kenn Duncan, the famous dance/theater photographer, in which Broadway stars posed in fantasy outfits all in white . . . except for their footwear, which was fire-engine red.

Like the Shubert Alley auction a dozen years later, Kenn's book raised a lot of money for charity. Last April, we threw a party for the cast of *The Visit* at home, and at one point, on our sofa sat Chita Rivera, Donna McKechnie, and Roger Rees—all three of whom posed in 1984 for *Red Shoes*.

By now, you're itching to know exactly what Roger's dream role was. It was a favorite of lots of boys from England, who found in our Wild West the lure of wide open spaces, big sky, fast horses, and exotic adventures: the American cowboy.

Roger in red cowboy boots as shot by Kenn
Duncan in 1984 for his book Red Shoes

Ride on, Rog! Ride on!
Lots of love,
Rick

HIRAETH

LAST NIGHT, I GOT TO SEE KATE BURTON and Dana Ivey and we were talking about Wales and the Welsh, which Kate famously is, and Roger's Welshness, so today—one month since Roger passed away—I thought I'd give you a sense of his people and his home.

Two Welsh friends, Kate Burton and Rog, while shooting Grey's Anatomy, *2007*

The Welsh side of Roger's family was his father's side.

Roger's grandfather, John Rees, and his grandmother, Mabel Lavinia Rees, did not have a happy marriage. At some point before 1910, Roger's gran left John in Aberystwyth on the west coast of Wales, took her baby, William John Rees (Roger's dad), and moved to Herefordshire, near Ross-on-Wye, settling in a small town called Sellack in the verdant Wye Valley. In Sellack, she met and fell in love with a handyman, Jack Voysey, and they lived together for the rest of their lives. Jack was the only grandfather Roger knew.

Roger's dad, Bill, grew into a pretty dashing fellow. He was a real personality in Sellack.

Roger's dad, William John Rees, in Sellack, 1926

Granny Mabel with her son, Bill, in Sellack, 1926

Roger's dad, Bill (left), and Jack Voysey mending a shed in Sellack, 1926

Roger's dad (left) on duty near the Lavender Hill station in London, 1929

Bill moved to London in 1927 at the age of twenty-three to make a life for himself. A few months later, he joined the police force in Lavender Hill.

Bill Rees got to be known around the neighborhood, and became a bit of a local hero after rescuing people from a burning building. Having thus established his reputation, he set his sights on Doris Louise Smith (who was known as Lucy).

They married and took a small flat in Clapham Junction in Battersea, South London. It was pretty basic: no indoor plumbing, a few chickens in the backyard. Roger was born in 1944, just a few weeks before the Allies stormed the beaches in France on D-Day.

Roger's mum, Doris Louise "Lucy" Rees, in Ramsgate, Kent, 1937

SIDEBAR:

Me, with Roger's mum, Lucy, forty years later on his fortieth birthday. Roger, Lucy, and I had a quiet celebration at her house in South London, because Rog had to be back up in Stratford the next day for a performance. But he wanted to be home with his mum on that special day.

Lucy and me in Wandsworth, South London, 1984

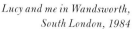

Back to our story. . . .

Roger, not quite two years old, visiting the countryside, Ross-on-Wye, 1946

Granny Mabel, Rog, and his mum, Lucy, 1946

Bill Rees continued to work for the London police at Lavender Hill when Rog was a tyke. They never missed an opportunity to travel to Herefordshire to visit Granny Mabel and "Grandpa" Jack.

Four years later, Andy, Roger's brother, was born.

Bill Rees and his son Roger, in Sellack, 1947

Rog (left) with his brother, Andy, in London, 1951

On June 2, 1953, Queen Elizabeth II was officially crowned. Bill was working during the Queen's coronation celebration. He was stationed on the Mall leading from Buckingham Palace to Westminster. It was a great honor to be given a post with such proximity to the Queen. Bill's job that day was to hold back the crowds. He had to face the mobs of adoring subjects, so even as the Queen's gilded coach clopped by within mere feet of him, Bill never got to see her; he was facing the other way, into the crowd. Bill, figuring everything after that would be downhill, retired from the force in late 1953.

Rog, age nine, in London, 1953

Roger was nine years old.

After retiring from the force, Bill Rees worked as a security guard. About this time, his heavy drinking was catching up with him. Drink started getting him into more and more trouble, and Bill found it hard to keep a job. Eventually, Rog remembered, his dad tried to make money with some crazy schemes.

One of these, Rog recalled vividly. Bill came home one day with a trunk containing eight thousand little plastic British soldiers. His job was to paint them: red coats, black trousers, brown rifles. "Can

Bill Rees, Roger's dad, on his sixtieth birthday. He died a year later.

you imagine?" Rog would say. "With all the drink in him, trying to paint those tiny soldiers? And for what—five for a penny? That lasted about half an hour."

The next chunk of years were marked by more fights between Bill and Lucy, and more distance between Rog and his dad. Rog retreated to the art room at school, where he could draw instead of talk. He was happier making himself scarce around the house, and he was good at art. By the time he was a teen, Rog had gotten himself a scholarship to the Slade School, sort of the Harvard and MIT of art schools. He was painting full time and felt like he'd found himself.

Roger's dad died suddenly when he was sixty-one years old. Rog always thought it was ironic that they were doing what Roger loved most, painting, when it happened. The stairs in the house needed a refresher coat of paint. Rog was at the top working his way down. Bill was at the bottom, painting the landing. Rog could hear his dad, breathing and brushing. Then, a moment later, the two sounds stopped. Rog came down the stairs, and his father was on his back, with paint spattered all over him.

Rog gave him the kiss of life, but it was too late. Bill's heart had stopped. Rog had to go down to the shop where his mother was working to give her the news.

When his dad died, Roger dropped out of art school and went to work to support his mother and his brother. A few years later, Andy had an important customer relations job at British Airways and was married to Carol Ambler. They had a passel of pets, the senior member of which was Newman, pictured right. Newman was named after Newman Noggs, the character from *Nicholas Nickleby*.

Newman, Carol Rees (Andy's wife), Andy (kneeling), and Rog in Bagshot, Surrey, 1983. Rog has his beard from The Real Thing.

We enjoyed long walks in the woods of Bagshot Park, near to where Andy and Carol lived in Surrey. It wasn't far from Heathrow. Rog and I spent the afternoon hiking with Andy and Carol before Rog deposited me at the airport for my flight to New York on Sunday evening.

In April 1989, I was over in London on a business trip while Roger was playing in *Hapgood* at the Doolittle Theatre in Los Angeles. I visited Lucy in South London for dinner, and Andy was off-duty from Heathrow, so he came by with Newman to say hello.

A month after this photo was taken, Lucy was in Los Angeles visiting Roger. Andy was house-sitting for his mum and, quite out of

Lucy with Giffard and Andy with Newman in Wandsworth, London, April 1989

the blue, had a seizure and died. Carol called Roger to give him the news. Rog and Andy were best friends, and Roger was devastated. Worse than that, Rog was left with the hardest thing he ever had to do: tell his mother and break her heart.

He kept putting it off, five more minutes, five more minutes; he just couldn't get the words out to tell her. There was a bluebird on the balcony, picking away at some birdseed that Lucy had just sprinkled around. *When the bird flies off, I'll tell her,* Roger thought.

I was in New York that day. Roger, bereft, called me. The bird had eaten its full and flown away. And Rog had just told his mother that her baby son had died. Arrangements needed to be made to return to London. It was a Sunday, Roger had a matinee—there was no understudy to go on—so Simon Jones's wife, Nancy, looked after Lucy while Roger, Simon, and Judy Davis played the play.

When the matinee was over, Roger and Lucy went right to the airport and flew home. I flew over the next day. I got to sit with Lucy, Roger, Carol, and Carol's parents, Ted and Vera Ambler, at Andy's funeral. He was only forty-one years old.

Roger stood and spoke Shakespeare's song from *Cymbeline*:

> *Fear no more the heat o' the sun,*
> *Nor the furious winter's rages;*
> *Thou thy worldly task hast done,*
> *Home art gone, and taken thy wages:*
> *Golden lads and girls all must,*
> *As chimney-sweepers, come to dust.*

Lucy held my hand so tightly while one of her sons spoke for the other. Six months later, on December 23, 1989, Lucy joined Bill and Andy up in heaven.

Almost twenty-six years later, when Rog was in the hospital with pneumonia in June, and I'd seen the last MRI report and knew how much his cancer had spread, I came home after midnight one night to shower and change my clothes and go back to be with Rog.

I passed this picture on the wall. The photo is from Roger's

Rog and his beloved mum, Lucy,
in Wandsworth, London, 1984

fortieth birthday, which we celebrated quietly with his mother. And I thought, *Soon, Lucy. You'll have his arms around you again soon.* Twenty days later, she did.

⊰⊱ ───── ⊰⊱

Hiraeth is one of those untranslatable Welsh words. It's sometimes used to mean homesickness, but Roger taught it to me as more powerful than mere nostalgic longing, more like a desperate, inexorable pull, a tugging deep in your heart to be in a mythical safe place with loved ones you have lost. It can't be avoided. You can try to tamp it down, but it will come back up in your heart and mind with more force. I don't think you have to actually be from Wales to know this feeling.

I'm not remotely Welsh, but I feel it. I think it's one of the things that helped me and Rog forge our connection—a longing for home, the struggle to get there, the joy that waits there, the safety that covers you there, wherever, whatever home is. It might be, simply and profoundly, in the arms of someone you love and who loves you.

When I look at Rog and his mother in this photo, when I see how happy they are together, I think the pull of *Hiraeth* has carried Rog from the home we shared to another place, from my arms to other arms that will hold him and love him. Hold him tight for me, Lucy.

Lots of love to Rog and Lucy and Andy and Bill, and Granny Mabel and "Grandpa" Jack, too.

And lots of love to all of you,
Rick

FROM SCENERY TO STAGE

A FEW PEOPLE SENT ME Linda Winer's *Newsday* column about Roger, wondering why a stage actor's stage credits generally come after the TV and/or film credits. Well, not wondering why—it's not hard to figure out—but wishing it were otherwise, especially when, as in Roger's case, there are scores of stage roles that might better describe that part of his life.

The dozens of crosswords that seize on REES for the lower right corner (usually) typically use clues like "*Cheers* actor Roger . . ." But here are some less typical clues to help define Mister Rees.

Starting out, Rog—like most of us—was just trying to fit in anywhere. He was in school, and it was a rough school, and Rog escaped into art . . . and started to draw.

He was also in the youngest level of Scouts, known as the Wolf Cubs.

Rog, in his Wolf Cub debut in 1951; he's immediately to the right and one row above the scowling Cubmaster, center.

Roger's second Wolf Cub troop, 1952. Roger is second from right in the middle row.

When he was nine years old, Rog graduated to a more colorful troop, becoming a full-fledged Scout.

Roger Rees, Scout, 1953. Once again, Rog is second from right in the middle row, edging his way toward center stage, an instinct that never left him.

Soon he began to appear in Scout productions, such as *Four and Twenty Blackbirds.*

Rog, age ten, in Four and Twenty Blackbirds; *luckily he was not in one of the title roles in this 1954 production.*

Roger's natural talent and his shapely legs were soon spotted, and the Scouts "jobbed him out" for shows at the Guildhall School of Music and Drama. Some of these productions were practically David Merrick-esque in scope.

Aladdin *(a 1955 pre-Disney version). Rog is four spears in from the left in the back row.*

Rog, second window from left with powdered wig, in a 1956 rendition of Cinderella

And then came the Gang Shows. Rog loved them.

SIDEBAR:

Ralph Reader was a British actor, producer, and songwriter who created the Gang Shows, variety entertainment presentations by members of the Boy Scouts throughout the United Kingdom. He also produced and choreographed West End productions, notably variety performances at the Drury Lane and the Hippodrome.

In 1932, Reader anonymously staged his first all-Scout variety show called *The Gang's All Here*. The show featured 150 Boy Scouts largely from London's East End performing sketches, songs, and dance numbers. The following year *The Gang Comes Back* played to capacity houses and the public and press began referring to, and clamoring for, what became known simply as The Gang Show.

In 1934, the title officially became *The Gang Show* and Reader billed himself as producer. Besides creating the Gang Shows, Reader, in 1936, wrote and directed a dramatic pageant called *The Boy Scout* with a cast of 1,500 Scouts, staged at Royal Albert Hall. That same year he wrote and played the lead in a feature film called *The Gang Show*, which premiered at the Lyceum Theatre in London—where Roger's dear friends, Tom Schumacher and Peter Schneider, mounted Julie Taymor's brilliant production of *The Lion King* in 1999 (and where it's been playing ever since).

The Lyceum was sacred to Roger because it's Henry Irving's theater, and Irving, the consummate actor/manager, was a theatrical icon for Roger. But when we arrived for opening night of *The Lion King*, Rog said, "This is the theater where Ralph's movie opened."

Reader was important in the life of any Boy Scout in the 1930s and 1940s, and became a household name during World War II as Gang Shows traveled one hundred thousand miles and played before three million servicemen.

By the time of Roger's generation, Ralph Reader was a Scout hero, and a national hero, too. Eventually, he was knighted by the Queen. In 2007, Rog attended a celebration of seventy-five years of Gang Shows. Many of his fellow Gang Show cast members are still Roger's friends, all these years later.

After World War II, Reader revived many of the shows he had produced before the war. He also began producing the London Gang Show in 1950 and wrote more songs and musical plays for the Scout Association. That's when Roger got to know him.

Rog is asking Ralph Reader a pointed question during a Gang Show confab in 1959.

But, in his real life—his non-showbiz life—Rog was gradually moving more and more into the art room and doing more and more art projects. His school, the Balham County Secondary Modern School,

Ralph Reader assigning lyrics to Gang Show teammates, including Rog, far left, 1962

Roger, during the Gang Show period, 1959

was a fierce place, populated increasingly with kids from the Caribbean and India. Everyone was poor. There were daily knife fights and lots of bullying. It was tough and no one was particularly interested in theatricals. Rog found salvation in art. And he was good.

So good, in fact, that he received a scholarship to Camberwell College of Art. Which was followed by a full scholarship to the Slade School of Fine Art—the sacred training ground for many of the great English artists. Duncan Grant, Dora Carrington, Derek Jarman, Keith Henderson, G. K. Chesterton, Stanley Spencer, Peter Snow—they all studied at the Slade.

Roger was really talented, good enough that people stole pieces from his portfolio. He was going to be a big-canvas painter like Anselm Kiefer or something. But in Roger's third year, his father died and he quit school to support his mother and brother. He did menial jobs like washing venetian blinds at Simpson's of Piccadilly, before a brief career as a scenery painter.

It was through Peter Snow's program in theater design at the Slade that Roger caught the attention of Nicholas Georgiadis, the great theater and ballet designer, who hired Rog to paint scenery at the Royal Ballet, including Kenneth MacMillan's *Sleeping Beauty* and *Romeo and Juliet* (which paired Rudolf Nureyev, who had just defected from the Soviet Union, with the about-to-retire Margot Fonteyn). The partnership rejuvenated Fonteyn's career and made Nureyev an international superstar.

Fonteyn and Nureyev in rehearsals for Romeo and Juliet, *1965*

To augment his income, Rog started painting scenery around the country. Later that year, he was on a paint frame forty feet above the stage at Wimbledon Theatre, down the road from where he lived, when he was approached by actor/manager Arthur Lane, who asked Rog to stop painting the scenery and play a role in *Hindle Wakes* by Stanley Houghton, a proto-feminist hit in Britain. Though the pay for acting was a bit less than for painting, Rog agreed to give it a try.

Soon he was doing Christmas pantos with variety legends like Arthur Askey and Roy Castle.

Arthur Askey, 1900–1982   *Roy Castle, 1932–1994*

Doing sketches with old hands like Arthur and Roy gave Rog a deep respect and an abiding love for variety artists. "I always thought," Rog would say, "that I was a short music hall comedian stuck in a leading man's body."

Bitten by the acting bug but completely untrained, Rog decided to audition for the RSC. They told him to go away because his voice was no good. So he applied for a job as an assistant stage manager/prop-maker at the Pitlochry Festival in Scotland.

One of the actors at Pitlochry had an ear infection, so Rog was suddenly playing Yasha in *The Cherry Orchard* and Bruno in *Dear Charles*, and lots of small parts.

Rog, right of center with mustache, in The Cherry Orchard *at the Pitlochry Festival, 1967*

His season in Pitlochry gave Roger the confidence to have his first head shots taken.

It also gave him the confidence, in 1967, to audition a second time for Trevor Nunn and John Barton at the RSC. This time, the RSC said yes. About a year later, Nunn took over as artistic director.

Once he was accepted into the RSC, Roger never looked back. Joining that company made him into a man. Here's proof:

And he never painted scenery again, gradually moving out of the shadows upstage and more and more into the light, down center.

In 1974, Rog made his Broadway debut at the Palace Theatre, playing in *London Assurance* with another of his heroes, the great Sir Donald Sinden (1923–2014).

SIDEBAR:

In October 2012, Donald hosted an event in Roger's honor at the Garrick Club in London. Garrick, you'll remember, is another of Roger's actor/heroes. It was such a happy night for Rog, sitting next to Sir Donald Sinden, directly under the huge portrait of David Garrick.

I was lucky enough to be there, too. It was a great night to stand next to *my* hero.

Rog and me at the Garrick Club on (where else?) Garrick Street in London, October 2012, surrounded by portraits of all of Roger's heroes—the great British actors

Here, in the role of Charles Courtly in the RSC production of *London Assurance* (directed by Ronald Eyre), is thirty-year-old Roger Rees, as he appeared on Broadway in December 1974.

Just for context (and giggles), here's a photo taken one year later, in December 1975. It's my first-ever head shot, taken for my upcoming audition for Yale Drama School. I was barely twenty years old, but, clearly, already inspired by Rog—or at least by his hair. . . .

Lots of love to everyone,
Rick

Me, Yale Drama School auditions, February 1976

ONE LITTLE YEAR

A YEAR AGO TODAY, ROGER FINISHED HIS RUN of *The Visit* at Williamstown. We woke up early, cleaned out his room, and packed up the car. We even managed a quick trip to the Clark Institute before the show (at right).

Roger posted this costume test by Ann Hould-Ward (below) on Facebook, just before the final performance of *The Visit*: "'And so ends the story of Anton Schell.' The last day (for now) of this lovely VISIT up here at Williamstown. What a pleasure to be in the room, onstage and in the wings with my snazzy and beautiful Chita, and English Rosie, John D, Terrence and Tom, John K, Graciela, David L, Jesse K, Harrison B, Libby U, Sam F, Andrew, Devin and Kirsten, John Bambery, Jason Danieley, Matthew Deming, Diana DiMarzio, Melanie Field, Davis Garrison, Rick Holmes, Judy Kuhn, Jude McCormick, Tom Nelis, Chris Newcomer, Aaron Ramey, Tim Shew, Michelle Veintimilla, the great and stylish designers, the brilliant crew and elecs, Josh Reid, and the astonishing superbly magnificent apprentices."

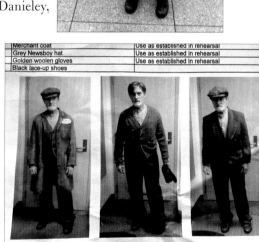

Merchant coat	Use as established in rehearsal
Grey Newsboy hat	Use as established in rehearsal
Golden woolen gloves	Use as established in rehearsal
Black lace-up shoes	

After we said good-bye to everybody—parting from Williamstown was difficult because Roger had put so much into his three years there as artistic director (2005–2007), and he loved the people and the building and the campus and the apprentices so much—we drove to the 1896 Pub on the road out of town to join Chita Rivera, her daughter, Lisa, her sister and brothers, and Rosie Bentinck, her assistant, for a farewell toast.

We left after one round because the forecast was for heavy rain, heading south and west into New York. Rog and I piled into the car and hit the road. Gradually, the sky turned from pink to gray, growing darker and darker. We were ten miles north of Poughkeepsie when it started drizzling. . . .

I don't like the Taconic Parkway in the rain. After a few minutes, it was teeming. We couldn't see a thing, even with the wipers on high. Rog said, "Maybe we should wait this out." I tried to find a place to pull over that didn't leave us too close to the road, too vulnerable for someone coming up behind us and not seeing us on the shoulder. Just the sound of the rain now, beating down on the roof, the hood, the windshield . . . *eine kleine nacht* tension on a Sunday evening. . . .

Eventually, the rain let up and we got back on the road. Rog held my hand for a minute. We had felt exposed on the side of the road, unprotected, and pretty near blind. It was good to be able to see again, to be able to drive again, and he reached for my hand and squeezed it.

A week later, we'd be back up the Taconic in Hillsdale, New York, visiting Tom Schumacher and Matthew White, and their dog, Holden— whom Rog had adored since he was a wee pup.

Roger and Holden in Hillsdale, New York, August 27, 2014

A week after that, Roger was in England, visiting his cousin, Betty Weeden.

Betty's husband, John, had died two months before, while Rog and I were in San Diego working on a show. So Rog flew over for some time with her, her son Jim, and Jim's family: Annabel, Hannah, and Molly.

Roger and Betty in Devon, England, September 5, 2014

Rog with his cousins, the Weedens: Jim (right) and his brother, Richard, are Roger's godsons.

Then he drove up to Sellack to visit the grave of his granny, Mabel Lavinia Rees, take a dip in the River Wye, and then drive back over to London to see some friends and a couple of shows, before heading home in time for . . . Rosh Hashanah 5775!

Rog with my brother, Michael, at our holiday dinner, with an amazing sunset behind them

Ten days later, we emerged from Yom Kippur services, hungry but atoned. . . .

Michael and JoAnn Elice, with Rog, outside Congregation Rodeph Sholom, ready to break the fast

Rog was so proud of his handstand! He did this one on October 1, 2014.

A week after that, Rog was back at work, taking tap classes with Crystal Chapman and doing Bikram yoga every morning.

In the afternoon, he'd learn his lines or write something, and then take a half-hour break to walk across the park to the museum and contemplate something beautiful.

And then, a few days later, Rog was diagnosed.

I don't know how something like that happens. I don't know how the man in these pictures, so happy, so full of life, could have, in these same pictures, something growing inside his head that would take him away from us . . . leaving me, one little year later, to chronicle his life—a life so rich and deep it beggars chronicling—instead of sharing a cup of coffee with him on the terrace, or driving home with him after a show at Williamstown. . . .

Rog at the Metropolitan Museum of Art in New York, October 3, 2014

The most precious gift our marriage gave me was the daily, palpable impact of a force—Roger—so strong, so intimate, so natural that it never occurred to me that it might not be there one day.

And now, I open my eyes and look for Rog, and my heart and body cry out, *Oh, my dear, my sweetheart, come back, come back! Just for a minute!* But I know this is impossible. Everything I loved is gone. The old life, the jokes, the long walks, the long talks, the loving, the partnering, the sharing. All of it, gone. Part of the past.

But that's all I want: the happy past restored.

The happy past—the two of us in 1992

And yet . . . that, just that, is what I ask for again when I go to bed, making sad, silent, middle-of-the-night bargains. Oh, what I'd do for a little more time with this man.

Lots of love to everyone,
Rick

TERRENCE MCNALLY /
A Speech at Roger's Memorial, New Amsterdam Theatre, September 21, 2015

I'm pretty certain I'm not the only person here today who had a crush on Roger. I wouldn't be surprised if everyone did. Iconic performances, such as his in *Nicholas Nickleby*, come once in a generation. And when they do, we all fall a little bit in love. It was an experience that remains seared in our collective memory of what great theater is. That's true immortality. Most of us would take that over a Hirschfeld or a Tony anytime.

Such a crush can be erotic, emotional, and moral. Mine was all three. He was a handsome devil, that's for sure. He was passionate, intelligent, sexy, and a little dangerous. He was the stuff bobby-soxers are made of. He must have been a Hamlet for the ages. It's New York's loss he never played it here.

Time was good to Roger. As he grew older, he became more beautiful. He became the essence of Roger. The youthful bravado gave way to a mature man of profound gravitas. The great roles that were awaiting him only deepen our sense of a life cut too short.

We had Roger's early fall. We were denied his deep winter.

As for the emotional crush—how could you not be taken by this young Nicholas, who wanted love and happiness so badly and did not rest until he found them. Nicholas's journey is every man's. For all those wonderful hours, we were *all* Nicholas Nickleby. And his name was Roger Rees. We were smitten beyond measure.

Years later, in *A Man of No Importance*, Roger was making the same hazardous journey, again without an ounce of self-pity, without a twinge of bitterness. His Alfie Byrne was a man without defenses in his desire to love and be loved. As with Nicholas, we knew Alfie because we recognized ourselves in him. Roger had a way of letting us in, without ever asking us to like him.

But his acting was only half the story. The rest was his humanity. His good looks had nothing to do with it. He could have played that part with a bag over his head, and we still would've fallen in love with him.

The journey ended this spring with *The Visit*. At the end of that show, Roger, playing Anton Schell, said, "I'm ready," and accepted his transformation from a deeply flawed and tragic man into an honorable and radiant one. In those two words— *I'm ready*—a man of no importance became a great man; one willing to die for our sins.

Standing at the back of the Lyceum Theatre, and knowing how sick he was, I died a little every time Roger said, "I'm ready." I know it's only a line from a script—"I'm ready"—but I think Roger *was* ready; showing the rest of us how it's done. We all knew the end was fast approaching, but we were the ones who weren't ready. Perhaps the purpose of art is to make us accept our mortality. If it is, Roger was a great teacher of the grace and serenity available to us when we put fear and pettiness behind us.

Nicholas Nickleby's journey ended triumphantly. For my money, so did Anton Schell's in *The Visit*. It is no accident the same actor played them both. My Roger crush had become profound respect and gratitude for a cherished friend and collaborator.

The moral crush is easier to explain. No actor played simple decency as effortlessly as Roger Rees. He personified it. Very few actors do. Decency—it's simply a word. We know when we're in the presence of it. We all just basked in Roger's. Even when the going got tough at the Lyceum—and it got very tough—Roger was more concerned about his fellow actors and what his failing health was doing to their performances than about his own ordeal. His cup of human kindness was infinite and bottomless. I hope he felt ours for him.

My favorite memory of Roger will always be seeing him in a men's room in Brooklyn, at a small theater company that was performing *A Man of No Importance*. Writers are notorious for traveling to Timbuktu for a production of one of their shows. But actors? When I challenged him on what the hell he was doing there, his response was cheerful and matter-of-fact. "I never saw the show. I was only in it. I wanted to see for myself."

That curiosity, that—especially with the actors who had no idea that the original Alfie Byrne was in the audience until after the performance—spontaneous and natural grace; these were pure Roger. I had chosen a wonderful man to have my crush on. Lucky Rick Elice. Lucky Roger Rees.

People who die before we think they should upset us with their passing. I still haven't been able to listen to the cast recording of *The Visit*. When I do, I know I'll hear Roger say, "I'm ready." It's easier writing these words than to hear his voice again. When I do, I'll know that those who leave us too soon try to teach us something by their leaving. That we, too, must be ready. Especially we who have chosen this least permanent of the arts for our life's work. We must realize that by giving our lives to it, we have perhaps helped others to be ready. Our lives in the theater are but a moment. Right now, Roger seems even less. He is gone. But his legacy isn't. He was an artist. That makes him immortal.

Thank you, Roger Rees, for your life and your artistry and your great kindness. You belong to the world now.

Thank you, Rick, for sharing him with us.

THE FAVORITE STAGE FIGHT

THE OTHER DAY, I RECEIVED A MESSAGE from Lily King Bodley, who, for four years, worked with Rog and Alex Timbers as their associate director on *Peter and the Starcatcher* at the New York Theatre Workshop on Broadway and for the first national tour.

Lily used to ask Rog about his RSC days, and Rog enjoyed telling her about the plays, the people, and his abiding belief in Shakespeare as a life guide.

SIDEBAR:

Trevor Nunn always said that Shakespeare has more to say about the human condition than the Bible. "Shakespeare has more wisdom and insight about our lives, about how to live and how not to live, how to understand our fellow creatures, than any religious tract," Trevor told *Christian Today* magazine in 2014. I think Rog probably agreed with him. He might have even gotten into that with Lily at the back of the theater one day. He certainly talked about it a lot with me. But I digress. . . .

Anyhow, Lily mentioned that one of her singular memories is the time she asked Roger what his favorite stage fight of all time was. Perhaps I should spell it *favourite* in light of Roger's answer, delivered with what Lily describes as his usual energetic-but-casual flair.

If you guessed Richard Cottrell's production of *Jack and the Beanstalk*—you'd be wrong, despite the gleeful visage in this photo.

Rog told Lily there was no question. "It was when I played Hamlet at the RSC . . ."

Roger as Idle Jack in Jack and the Beanstalk *at the Cambridge Theatre Company in 1973*

The famous Philip Core poster for the RSC's Hamlet *in 1984*

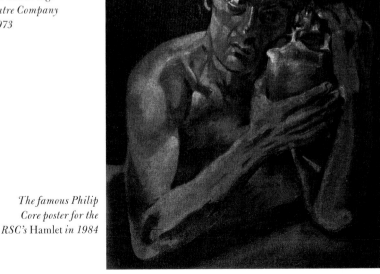

HAMLET

". . . and, for quite a few minutes in the final scene—and this was a three-plus-hours production, mind you—I had to fight Ken Branagh's Laertes, during which we—and several other key characters—were mortally wounded. And the stage was RAKED!"

Rog slicing into Ken Branagh's back in the final scene of the RSC's production of Hamlet

This production of *Hamlet* was directed by Ron Daniels, who had directed Rog in the RSC's smash hit production of *The Suicide* by Nikolai Erdman in 1979. Ken Branagh was Laertes, Frances Barber was Ophelia, Brian Blessed was Claudius, Virginia McKenna was Gertrude, Frank Middlemass was Polonius, Richard Easton was the Ghost, and Nick Farrell was Horatio. The production was designed by Maria Bjornson, who perfected, in this *Hamlet*, the use of huge swags of curtains as visual "wipes"— a technique she employed to great effect in the very next show she designed: Andrew Lloyd Webber's *The Phantom of the Opera*, now the longest-running show in the history of the whole world ever.

And as long as I'm digressing . . .

Here's a shot of Roger in rehearsal, practicing the spectacular sword fight at the climax of the play.

Roger in rehearsal for Hamlet

The eagle-eyed among you will note that, in the photo on the preceding page, Roger's T-shirt says WITTENBERG U. This was Roger's little joke; Hamlet is a student at Wittenberg University when he is called home for his father's funeral and, immediately after, his mother's *o'erhasty* marriage to his uncle. So Rog liked to wear his "Uni Tee" for rehearsals. Digression ends.

Over the past few weeks, I've heard from so many people who saw Rog play Hamlet. I saw it myself twenty-five times over the course of a year and a half. And Rog was quite right—the fight with Laertes was incredibly good, intricate, brutal, breathtaking, and utterly convincing. Even with the raked stage. Or, maybe, in part, *because* of the steep rake, courtesy of the brilliant Maria Bjornson.

When Rog was onstage, ready for the fight ("The readiness is all"), he looked like this:

Rog as the Prince of Denmark, 1984

When he left the theater after playing Hamlet, with his sore calves and twisted tendons from the raked stage, Rog still somehow managed to look like this.

Rog at the RSC Stage Door in Stratford-upon-Avon, 1984

Roger played Hamlet for nearly 150 performances, in Stratford-upon-Avon and later at the Barbican in London. Indeed, the production proved so popular it was honored (fine, *honoured*) with this magazine cover.

Thanks for the message, Lily! Keep hearing Roger's voice, and the notes, and the jokes—ah, the old jokes—and the stories, the wonderful stories. The stories keep him alive.

Lots of love to everyone,
Rick

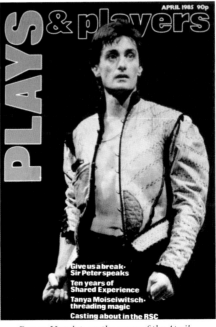

Rog as Hamlet, on the cover of the April 1985 Plays & Players *magazine*

A MUSE OF FIRE

FACT IS, I HADN'T THOUGHT ABOUT WRITING anything today, August 26, because it's our anniversary, mine and Rog's, and it's a sad day for me . . . one of the "firsts" as they're called in bereavement groups. The first birthday, the first Thanksgiving, the first anniversary. You get the drift. So I thought I'd spare you my moping. Also, it's the anniversary of our marriage, but we were only able to get married four years ago, when such a thing was at last deemed legal in New York State. Rog and I have always celebrated our anniversary on September 23— the night of our first date, our first kiss . . . the night after the fateful dress rehearsal of *Cats*—when we first met and spoke to each other.

A public garden on West Eighty-Ninth Street, between Columbus and Amsterdam Avenues, as seen in March 2012

From the Royal Botanic Gardens in downtown Sydney, photographed September 2010

But last night, Dan Doniger, the registered nurse from Calvary Hospice who looked after Roger in the last weeks of his life, came by to visit. It's remarkable, after the fact, to still be in contact with Henry Friedman, the remarkably kind doctor from Duke, and Dan Doniger, the sweet and stalwart nurse from Calvary. It's a testament to their goodwill and commitment, certainly.

Dan and I were chatting, and I mentioned that today was our anniversary, and he asked me how I was going to observe it. I was stymied. I planned no observance other than to be sad, to keep busy through the day, and visit a friend in the evening so I wouldn't be home alone. And Dan said that was one way to do it. (He never comes out and says, *You're wrong, here's what you should do.*) But then he asked me what we'd have done, Rog and me, if we were together. How would we celebrate the day? Would we go out for a meal, would we take a trip, what would we do?

And I said, "Well, probably all that would have happened

Lilacs in London, spring 2008

191

is that I would have filled the apartment with flowers and then, in the O. Henry way in which our lives frequently unfolded, Roger would arrive with additional armfuls of flowers and we'd have flowers overflowing in every room."

Dan said, "Why don't you do that for him? Why don't you observe the day for Roger?"

I decided that Dan was quite right, so I'm sending this report to you—his friends and loved ones—full of images of what Roger loved best: nature's bounty.

From our terrace, summer 2013, homegrown!

Tropical plants actually in the tropics! Photographed in Hawaii, summer 2009.

SIDEBAR:

The photo opposite was taken when my nephew, Jeremy Elice, married the magnificent Nicole Caprio on August 29, 2009, at Turtle Bay Resort on Oahu.

Rog and I bumped into Jeremy and Nic on the morning of their wedding. They were going for a run. We were on our way to the all-you-can-eat buffet.

Nicole and Jeremy, burning calories

After breakfast, Rog did one of his top three favorite things: he found a stable, chose a horse, changed into long pants, and went for a canter down the beach.

Rog and a new friend, sizing each other up

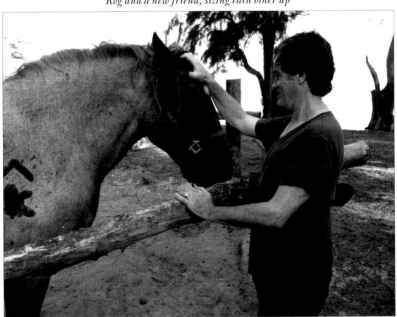

Later that day, we all celebrated the big event.

*Nicole and Jeremy, newly married,
August 29, 2009*

It was a great wedding and a great trip.

It's important to me and Rog to share this anniversary report with Jeremy and Nicole—and their beautiful daughter, Vivi—as their sixth wedding anniversary approaches this weekend. We love you guys!

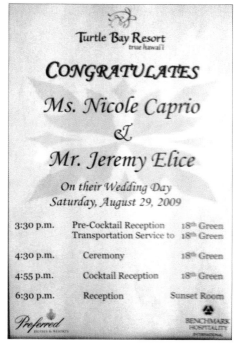

Turtle Bay Resort
true hawai'i

CONGRATULATES

Ms. Nicole Caprio
&
Mr. Jeremy Elice

On their Wedding Day
Saturday, August 29, 2009

3:30 p.m.	Pre-Cocktail Reception	18th Green
	Transportation Service to	18th Green
4:30 p.m.	Ceremony	18th Green
4:55 p.m.	Cocktail Reception	18th Green
6:30 p.m.	Reception	Sunset Room

Preferred
HOTELS & RESORTS

BENCHMARK
HOSPITALITY
INTERNATIONAL

Jeremy, Vivi, and Rog in Los Angeles, June 2014

The riot of nasturtiums on our terrace after Rog came home from the hospital, July 4, 2015

But I digress. . . .
Back to our House of Flowers.

In addition to armfuls of flowers, Rog would present me with one or two of his "quick shots"—oft told, ever-delightful items from Roger's stash of stories—told and retold year after year, grown more ridiculous with repetition, but always fun. Today, for this year's anniversary, they're comforting

Me and Rog, during Christmas in London, 1983

in their familiarity. They bring back happy memories of Rog and me, me and Rog, over the years.

Rog had a few dozen of 'em at his fingertips, but two that spring to mind are these. Imagine Roger recounting them, and you will hear him. It's ever so much better when he tells it:

> Sir John Gielgud appeared in a production of *Oedipus* at the National Theatre in London during the 1968 season. The audience, upon arriving, was greeted by a gigantic golden phallus thirty feet high, towering over the stage.
>
> On opening night, the actress Coral Browne entered the theater and looked up for a long moment. Then she turned to her companion and said, "No one I know!"

Together in Tokyo, October 1984

And:

In 1982, Rog went to France to make a film called *Imaginary Friends* with Peter Ustinov and Lili Palmer. He had a blast listening to Ustinov— one of the all-time great raconteurs—raconteuring every night at the hotel where the actors were billeted. This was his favorite Ustinov story:

> Peter Ustinov wrote a play called *The Moment of Truth* in 1951, at the height of the Actors Studio fame, courtesy of Marlon Brando and his fellow method actors.
>
> Ustinov was watching a rehearsal and lost his temper with a particularly tiresome practitioner of the "method." So he stood in the aisle and shouted at the man onstage: "Don't just do something—stand there!"
> *(RIMSHOT, no doubt!)*

I've listened with delight as Rog dusted off these little nuggets through the years. . . .

London, Christmas of 1985

Up in British Columbia,
Canada, October 1994

Out in Los Angeles,
August 1999

In New York, Christmas 2005

New York at the Tony Awards, June 2012

New York, on Thanksgiving 2014

Just before his second brain surgery, New York, March 2015

At holidays and special occasions like anniversaries, there would also invariably be an evocation of Shakespeare, or an invocation of blessing—such as this from *A Midsummer Night's Dream*:

OBERON
> *Through the house give glimmering light*
> *By the dead and drowsy fire;*
> *Every elf and fairy sprite*
> *Hop as light as bird from brier;*
> *And this ditty after me,*
> *Sing and dance it trippingly.*

TITANIA
> *First, rehearse your song by rote,*
> *To each word a warbling note:*
> *Hand in hand, with fairy grace,*
> *Will we sing, and bless this place.*

And then, last of all, Rog would say this, from *Henry V*. It was always spoken like an incantation, binding both of us, separately and together, to a life in the theater. Imagine being me, alone with Roger Rees in a room overflowing with books, remains of dinner on the table, volumes various and sundry open here and there, and my very own personal prologue, my sweet Shakespearean scholar, speaking thus:

> *O! for a Muse of fire, that would ascend*
> *The brightest heaven of invention;*
> *A kingdom for a stage, princes to act*
> *And monarchs to behold the swelling scene.*
> *Then should the war-like Harry, like himself,*
> *Assume the port of Mars; and at his heels,*
> *Leash'd in like hounds, should famine, sword, and fire*
> *Crouch for employment. But pardon, gentles all,*
> *The flat unraised spirits that hath dar'd*
> *On this unworthy scaffold to bring forth*
> *So great an object: can this cockpit hold*

The vasty fields of France? or may we cram
Within this wooden O the very casques
That did affright the air at Agincourt?
O, pardon! since a crooked figure may
Attest in little place a million;
And let us, ciphers to this great accompt,
On your imaginary forces work.
Suppose within the girdle of these walls
Are now confin'd two mighty monarchies,
Whose high upreared and abutting fronts
The perilous narrow ocean parts asunder:
Piece out our imperfections with your thoughts:
Into a thousand parts divide one man,
And make imaginary puissance;
Think when we talk of horses that you see them
Printing their proud hoofs i' the receiving earth;
For 'tis your thoughts that now must deck our kings,
Carry them here and there, jumping o'er times,
Turning the accomplishment of many years
Into an hourglass: for the which supply,
Admit me, Chorus, to this history;
Who prologue-like your humble patience pray,
Gently to hear, kindly to judge, our play.

Heaven.

Happy anniversary, my love.

And lots of love to everyone,
Rick

Together in New York,
November 1983

RICK ELICE /
A Speech at Roger's Memorial, New Amsterdam Theatre, September 21, 2015

I'd like to ask you to join me in wishing Roger's father-in-law a HAPPY BIRTHDAY. Harold Elice is eighty-eight years old today!

Thank you all for coming today, and thanks to everyone who participated. And thanks especially to Tom Schumacher and my friends at Disney Theatrical, and Nancy Coyne and my friends at Serino Coyne, for pulling the whole thing together. This would not have happened without them.

December 5, 1981. Since that day, I've been most wonderfully and completely in love with Roger Rees. The miracle of my life is that he loved me, too. And we were able to have many years of extreme happiness together.

On that long-ago day, December 5—which is a little eerie, because it's not only Tom Schumacher's birthday (and he's our gracious host this afternoon), but it's also Walt Disney's birthday, so you know . . . spooky. But on that long-ago day in 1981, I did the unthinkable. I paid *a hundred dollars* to see a Broadway show. Imagine anything so ridiculous.

Inside, the actors were milling about, mingling with the audience before the show started. I saw one of them, way down front. I didn't know who he was or what role he played. It turned out to be Roger Rees and he was playing Nicholas Nickleby. And I thought he was the most devastatingly beautiful person I'd ever seen.

The front of Jove himself,
An eye like Mars to threaten and command,
A station like the herald Mercury,
New-lighted on some heaven-kissing hill;
A combination and a form indeed,
Where every god did seem to set his seal
To give the world assurance of a man.
This was my husband.

. . . is probably a better way to put it. You've heard a lot about him today.

But what was he really like, this Roger Rees fellow? Well . . .

Roger was never happier than when he was surrounded by plants. He was never happier than when he was surrounded by books. He was never happier than when he was surrounded by friends. He was never happier than when he was surrounded by actors.

Roger was never happier than when he was at home. He was never happier than when he was traveling. He was never happier than when he was onstage. He was never happier than when he was backstage.

Roger was never happier than when he was painting. He was never happier than when he was writing.

He was never happier than when he was building something. Or solving something. Or making something.

Roger was a worker, and he was never happier than when he was working.

Roger was, therefore, basically always happy. And kind. Kind and happy.

What was Roger like? He was like *that*.

On the day he died, just ten weeks ago—Roger was still happy. He was weak and short of breath, but his mind was at peace. He knew what I hope you know: that he lived a good and worthwhile life. I know it was eight o'clock, curtain time, and he didn't exit here as much as made his entrance somewhere else.

But it was also Friday evening. The Sabbath had just begun. And as the Sabbath began, he rested. He loved and was loved. He gave and gave and was given much in return. He read and painted and planted and traveled and wrote and directed and mentored and performed. He worked. He knew to live such a life was a great privilege. He knew that to create was his great gift. And it was the Sabbath, and his work was done, and, in good conscience, he rested.

I am humbled by what we had, happy for what we did, sorry for what we didn't get to do, sad for what we lost, and proud of what we were: a happy couple more in love every year as the years went by. A grand passion.

That, of course, is the very thing I'm mourning for, homesick for, famished for. My mind tells me, Roger's passed on. But my heart and my body are crying out, "Come back, come back."

I know this is impossible. I know that the thing I want is exactly the thing I can never get. The old life, the jokes, the meals, the shows, the lovemaking, the tiny, heartbreaking commonplaces.

It's all gone. Part of the past. And the past is the past—but that's no consolation. A life is never taken away and given back. Yet that, just that, is what I cry out for, with middle-of-the-night endearments and questions asked of the empty air. As he was my guide, I am lost. As he was my fire, I am cold. As he was my strength, I am weak. But, as he was my partner, my teacher, my heart, my home, I am more than I had any hope of ever being without Roger Rees.

You might think it's all me, the man standing here talking to you. But that's only because, like all good directors, Roger was careful not to make his signature larger than the painting. The fact is, this "painting" is all him. What was Roger like? He was a really good director.

Of course, we know Rog best as an actor. So to know what he was really like, he'd want me to give you some context on the actor front.

It wasn't legal to bury an actor in Manhattan until 1890—before that they were buried in Queens with the sailors. In the Cemetery of the Evergreens in Glendale, there are five thousand indigent seamen from twenty-eight nations, and eight hundred actors—all getting along famously, I'm certain. And, quite right, too. They may not be historically well respected, but they're a friendly lot, this clutch of artists we call actors. They're heroic, too—the beating heart and bleeding feet, the sprained muscles and ragged throats, the tormented psyches and mind-blowing talents at the heart of holy rooms like this one.

Maybe they complain a bit when they're out of work. And when they're employed, maybe they're still a bit too easily dissatisfied. I guess the grass seems even greener on the other side of the greenroom. And yes, maybe they're a bit emotionally confused, sometimes maybe even a little schizo.

But it's the nature of the beast, right? Actors flit and flutter about. They're glorious, particular, beautiful, almost godlike creatures and they live for just a day. Roger was like *that*.

He wasn't educated in any formal sense of the word. When eventually he became an actor, he did so without ever having set foot in a drama school. "As any of you who've seen me perform can vouchsafe," Roger would say. But of course he was a wonderful actor.

He spent most of his early career at the Royal Shakespeare Company not saying a word, just holding a spear in the dark. Rog and his friend Ben Kingsley auditioned together and joined the RSC on the same day in 1967.

Their first parts were as silent, unlit huntsmen in *The Taming of the Shrew*. They were so good at this, they went on to play silent, unlit huntsmen in almost every Shakespeare play, learning their trade night after night, stumbling about, saying nothing—in what Rog called his "four years as a mime artist with the RSC."

It meant everything to Rog to be in that great company—so much that on the day he was finally given a speech to speak, they had to take it back again, because Rog was too nervous to say it.

Many years later, both Sir Ben—as he is now called— and Roger—still just plain Roger—had served their apprenticeships, and each of them got to play Hamlet. By then, of course, Rog had gotten quite good at speaking—and he was delighted to discover that Hamlet speaks. Quite a lot.

"A combination and a form indeed, where every god did seem to set his seal to give the world assurance of a man."

. . . that's Hamlet, I like to think, on the subject of Rog.

About that "Sir Ben"—Roger was never knighted. I think it's because he loved Americans too much. One American in particular.

Also, he made the knighthood-killing choice twenty years ago to play Prince Charles on a rather unfortunate television miniseries—*Unhappily Ever After.* It wasn't very good. And the royal family does not forgive bad television. Except, on occasion, their own.

But as it turned out, three years ago, Rog was back in London doing his one-man show about Shakespeare called *What You Will.* And Prince Charles came to see it—apparently the miniseries debacle had been forgotten.

After the show, Roger shook hands with Prince Charles—and then we headed off to the Garrick Club for a dinner in Roger's honor. On the way, Rog said, "I just shook hands with a man who shook hands, as a boy, with Winston Churchill—who shook hands with someone who'd shaken hands with Queen Victoria—and so on and on, and if you trace it back—I bet we've all shook hands with Shakespeare."

Yes—Shakespeare was Roger's other grand passion. What fascinated him most about the man, what inspired him most, was this: to himself, the Bard of Avon was not THE BARD OF AVON—or even a bibulous character played by Christian Borle in a Broadway musical. He was a guy who worked really hard. A man who wore the equivalent of sneakers and Levi's, sporting a smile or frown about the way the world wagged each day, taking his place in a long, long line of workers.

Roger was in that line right up to the end. "Why be finished?" he'd say. "Where's the fun in that? Great cities are never finished. Nothing sits. Except your dog—and look how anxious he is to get on with things."

To Roger, perfection was a moving point. He liked the pursuit. He sprinted after perfection every day till the day he ran out of breath. It seemed to him that he never got anything so right that he should no longer work to make it better.

At the end of his life, Rog said that he felt just like Oliver Twist, asking for one more go. "Please, sir, can I have some more?"

Dickens or Chekhov, Shakespeare or Sondheim, McNally or Miranda—take all the poetry away, and they're just men—who work. Hard. What was Roger like? He was like *that*.

I want to tell you about two young girls, who met each other a hundred years ago. One of the girls was Roger's grandmother, Mabel Lavinia Rees.

Born at the end of the nineteenth century, Mabel Lavinia was a country girl, never educated, but because she'd managed, at the age of fifteen, to find a job as a parlormaid in a grand country estate, she was much envied.

While working very hard in a large and imposing house, Mabel began an unprecedented friendship with the daughter of the rich and aristocratic family that lived there. These two very different young women, Roger's grandma and the daughter of the house, Elizabeth Rudd, remained dear friends all their lives. Think *Downton Abbey*, without the fund-raising breaks.

With Mabel's death in 1959 came REST AFTER TOIL—as it says on her grave in the country. Miss Rudd, who had become a respected justice of the peace, looked out for Roger as Mabel had asked, and was tremendously supportive of his career.

Rog was very keen that I should meet her. Miss Rudd was ninety-something years old by then, very frail, nearly blind, but we sat in the sun, high on a hill in Herefordshire, with a prospect down to the river. She asked me about my work ethic. Then she turned to Rog and gave me the thumbs-up, which pleased Roger very much. Me too.

When Miss Rudd died in 1986, she bequeathed us an old Chippendale desk at which she wrote Roger many letters over the years, and three or four to me.

It's in our apartment now, this desk. It has a couple of secret drawers. One day while cleaning the desk, Roger opened a compartment that he had never noticed before and found a poem.

The poet was a man called Babcock. Maltbie Davenport Babcock.

From the Monty Python-esque name, we assumed he was an eccentric Scotsman. But it turns out he was pastor of the Brick Church in Lower Manhattan from 1900 to 1901—just one year. He died, a short time later, working hard for his particular God, in the Holy Land.

Maltbie had a reputation for writing hymns and inspirational poems. But tell me—of all the poems ever written, why did Miss Rudd hide this particular one in her desk? Maybe she was thinking of her hardworking friend, Roger's Granny Mabel. Maybe she recognized something of Roger in the verse's call to action. Maybe Elizabeth Rudd, justice of the peace, sitting in the gloaming just across the hill from Wales, put that poem in that desk decades ago so that we could hear it in this theater today.

Things can come pretty well full circle if you've no idea what you're doing. One religion calls it karma—I call it having no idea what I'm doing. But Rog would say, "Rick, Rick, Rick. Try to do a thing without worrying too much about where you're going with it. Could you try that? For me?"

Okay, Rog. For you.

What was Roger really like? "Let it all go, that it might come back. Work like crazy. Bend with the wind. Embrace change. Welcome obstacles. Work like crazy. Be certain of nothing. Be bad sometimes. Never grow brittle. Never finish. Work like crazy."

Roger was like *that*.

Here's Maltbie Davenport Babcock's poem—from Miss Rudd . . . to Roger . . . to all of us:

We are not here to play, or dream, or drift.
We have work to do and loads to lift.
Shun not the struggle. Face it.
For work is life's greatest gift.

Say not the times are wicked,
Seek not someone to blame.
Don't fold your hands; Stand up, speak out,
and bravely stake your claim.

It matters not how deep-entrenched the wrong;
How hard the battle; the day, how long.
Faint not, fight on! Today, we work!
Tomorrow comes the song.
Tomorrow comes the song.

YAHRZEIT

JEWS REMEMBER FAMILY MEMBERS who are no longer with us by lighting candles that burn for twenty-four hours. This observance is called *Yahrzeit*—which means literally "anniversary candle." They are lit on the anniversary of death, and also on Yom Kippur. Roger's first Yahrzeit candle is today, Yom Kippur, September 23, 2015. I'd like to share an uncanny coincidence with all of you, while the sounds and sights of Roger's memorial on Monday still reverberate.

In 1982, on September 22, the final dress rehearsal for a new musical from London called *Cats* took place at the Winter Garden Theatre.

I was working at Serino Coyne (& Nappi, then)—as a part-time copywriter, having filled in for Nancy Coyne that summer while she was on vacation, and I was acting up a storm in *The Death of Von Richthofen as Witnessed from Earth*, a musical produced by Joe Papp, written and directed by some boy genius from Canada named Des McAnuff.

When Nancy returned from vacation, we hit it off and she kept me on, part-time. (The company was small then, no more than a dozen people.) *Cats* was the big fall opening, with previews starting on September 23.

The day before, a Wednesday, Nancy, who had already seen *Cats* in London, said, "You should go to the dress rehearsal tonight, because there are no tickets for previews. Take Hal." ("Hal" was Hal Luftig— yes, *that* Hal Luftig; an intern who would become a Tony Award– winning producer of note.)

So Hal and I walked up Broadway to the Winter Garden to see *Cats*.

As (my) luck would have it, Roger Rees happened to be there, too.

The next day, we had our first date. It was September 23, 1982.

Exactly one year earlier, September 23, 1981, *Nicholas Nickleby* played its first performance on Broadway. Exactly thirty-three years later, I'm writing this to you. But I'd like to tell you a bit about that Thursday night, September 23, 1982.

Rog was late. Very late. As in the-food-was-inedible late. I couldn't stand pacing in the one room, so I gave up and went down to the lobby and waited for him there. When he eventually showed up, he confessed that he almost didn't come at all; he was afraid I was a stalker. Eventually, and after a couple of whiskeys, he decided what the hell.

The rest of the evening was remarkably comfortable. We chatted our way across the street to a diner and picked up a couple of sandwiches, since the *croute* had been reduced to rubble. We chatted our way upstairs to my flat-ette. We talked some more as we ate the sandwiches, took turns playing the piano, made out a little, and listened to records and each other until four in the morning.

Roger invited me to walk him back to a friend's place across the street from the Morgan Library, so he could pick up his things before heading to the airport. We passed a mob of predawn rats skittering through Bryant Park. Rog said, "We should make tonight our anniversary, and remember these rats." It was the most romantic thing I'd ever heard.

An hour later, Rog piled into a car to go to JFK. He dropped the window and said, "Maybe you'll come over in six weeks and see me in *The Real Thing*. Here's my phone number in London." I told him there was no way I could afford international phone calls.

"Then here's my address. Write. Write a lot. Write me lots of letters. I'll write back."

I didn't go home. I sat with the rats in Bryant Park, celebrating my bad luck. I mean, how was I supposed to ever see this person again? He lived in London. He worked in London. And I, as my grandmother used to say, didn't have two nickels to rub together. But somehow, I wasn't unhappy. I was deliriously hopeful.

Thirty-three years ago. Today.

Yom Kippur is the holiest day of the Jewish year. It occurs on a different day every year, because the Hebrew calendar is based on the lunar cycle. Last year, for example, it was on October 4. Next year, it'll be on October 12. This year, it's September 23. Today.

How can it be that this year Yom Kippur would fall on September 23, our anniversary? How can it be that I'm lighting Roger's first *Yahrzeit* on the anniversary of our first kiss? Dear God, help me with this. Help me, please. The symmetry—fearful symmetry, is that what Blake called it?—it's like a knife in my heart.

And now, it's several hours later. The bright, sunny morning of September 24, 2015 . . . and I just got home from the dentist to finish this report. His name is Dr. Barry Sporer; he's Roger's dentist. I cracked a tooth last night, so this morning I took the subway to his office.

I came up from the subway at the corner of Bryant Park. And I realize I'm standing exactly where Rog and I stood in the predawn, rat-happy hours of September 24, 1982. I know I didn't plan this—certainly not the cracked-tooth part. But I'm precisely where I was, precisely thirty-three years ago. . . .

Before things start getting too weird, I'm calling a **SIDEBAR**:

Well, this is really a *downstage center bar*. It's to thank everyone who participated in Roger's memorial on Monday, September 21. Tom Schumacher (who very graciously handed over his magnificent New Amsterdam Theatre), and I had a good old chuckle over how crowded the theater was. I never imagined the huge place would be packed.

I want to thank the people who came from faraway places, like Dave Barry and Bob Gaudio; Alan Siegel and David Meister; Linda Kerns and James Warwick; Kate Burton and Finty Williams; and Danielle Robinson and Rodney Rigby. Let them stand in for all the names I'm forgetting. But people came from all over, which makes me so proud for Rog.

Everyone seems to think the memorial was extraordinary. That's mostly because Rog is extraordinary. But events don't just happen, so I want to thank the people who put the presentation together and made it so memorable. The creative supervision of Jeff Lee, Alex Timbers, Patrick McCollum, Lily King, Marco Paguia, Wayne Barker, and Ted Sperling. The stage management of Clifford Schwartz, Jason Trubitt, McKenzie Murphy, Samantha Preiss, and Terry Witter. The esteemed group of onstage performers: the choral ensemble of Master Voices, Marty Moran, Tom Schumacher, Heidi Blickenstaff, Christian Borle, Kate Burton, Mark Linn-Baker, Dana Ivey, Bebe Neuwirth, Scott Cady, Marshall Brickman, Sherie Renee Scott, Lindsay Mendez, Marco Paguia, Nancy Coyne, Terrence McNally, Chita Rivera, Michael Patrick Walker, Finty Williams, and John Caird. And finally, the teeming cast members from *Peter and the Starcatcher*. Thank you all.

A couple of people surprised me by showing up at the memorial, and one of them, Barry Edelstein, artistic director of The Old Globe in San Diego, wrote me this today:

When I was a graduate student at Oxford, I used to take the rickety, single-carriage train to Stratford to see plays. There was a bookstall in the lobby with a

rack of postcards of famous productions, and my favorite of all was of Roger as Hamlet, in the "Now might I do it pat" scene, pointing a rapier at the back of the kneeling Brian Blessed's neck. I love that photo.

Something about Roger's eyes. The hatred, the fear. The certainty, the doubt.

"Now might I do it pat!" / Rog as Hamlet, and Brian Blessed as Claudius

Something about that jaw and those cheekbones, hollowed by loss, yet strong with resolution. And the size of the gesture: visceral and vivid and indelible.

On the first day of rehearsal for The Misanthrope *at Classic Stage Company, I told the assembled cast about that photo, and the awe I felt that the actor in that photo was there, in the theater I ran, in the show I was directing.*

Every night at half hour he'd come into the most wretched dressing room in New York and make it his business to check in with every other actor: How are you? What's new? What happened to you today? What can we do to make tonight great? *It was the first time that I really understood why we call the main role in a play* the lead. *That actor is the leader, the guy who sets the tone for the company, who takes responsibility for morale and purpose and mission.*

Roger never carried himself like the theater god he was. He was always humble, gracious, courteous. Generous to me, a kid whom he knew had stars in his eyes, and to everyone in the company and on the theater's staff and board. And to the public. My goodness, he was amazing in that show! So funny, so precise, so intense! How lucky I was to be part of that.

One time I went to visit him backstage at Indiscretions *with Jude Law. His dressing room had surprisingly few photos and cards. A picture of Rick, of course, and a large picture of the cast of* Star Trek: The

Next Generation, *which had only just begun airing. I said, "Roger, I had no idea you liked* Star Trek.*"

"I don't," he explained. "Pat Stewart and I are mates." He said he was so proud of his old friend that he had to have a photo nearby at all times. "We did all right," Roger said, "though I'm in a clapped-out dressing room with banging pipes and he's on the bridge of a starship."

—**Barry Edelstein**

That same Patrick Stewart also turned up at Roger's memorial. Yesterday, he wrote me this very informative follow-up, which gives context to Roger's "four years as a mime artist with the RSC."

What a glorious curtain call you gave your husband and my friend. I have never experienced anything in such an event quite so filled with love, affection, humour, and admiration. I felt very special sitting there in that outrageous auditorium. Special because I know my love of Roger probably predated anyone present. I was onstage, generally making a mess as Grumio, when Roger and Sir Ben were background in The Shrew.

Pat Stewart as Grumio, Michael Williams as Petruchio, and Janet Suzman as Katherina in The Taming of the Shrew, *an RSC 1967 production*

Susan Fleetwood as Audrey and Pat Stewart as Touchstone in As You Like It, *1968*

By the next production, they both graduated from Huntsmen to Forest Lords in As You Like It. *Sir Ben sang, but Roger, I think, was still silent. Then at the end of that season came Trevor's* Revenger's Tragedy, *when I think both might have had a line or two. That is the production that catapulted Trevor into the limelight, and we were all hanging on to his coattails. A year later he was made artistic director.*

—**Patrick Stewart**

SIDEBAR ENDS. (That was some sidebar.)

MORE COINCIDENCES?

At the memorial two days ago, I was the final speaker. I told a little story about Roger's grandmother, Mabel Lavinia Rees. She's the one who worked as a parlormaid (she'd have said "parlourmaid") in a grand country estate in Herefordshire. The daughter of that house, Miss Elizabeth Rudd, became friends with Mabel. In the 1920s, Miss Rudd was forced to leave the house because, as a female, she couldn't inherit the estate. She moved to the other side of the valley, and Mabel no longer worked for her, but the two women stayed friends until Mabel Lavinia Rees died in 1959. By then, Rog was a teen, and he'd spent lots of time with Granny Mabel and Miss Rudd on those Herefordshire hilltops.

Miss Rudd took a great interest in Rog all his life. She even met me. As I said at the memorial, when she died at the age of ninety-six, she left Rog and me some furniture, including a desk in which Roger found a poem. To me, the poem glorifies a work ethic that personifies Granny Mabel, Miss Rudd, and Rog.

Anyhow, when I got home later that day, from having spoken about Rog and Mabel Lavinia Rees, I brought in the mail and noticed an envelope from England. It was from a grave maintenance company in Herefordshire that Rog hired to keep Granny Mabel's grave in good condition.

Inside was a photo (see below): the grave of the woman from Herefordshire, about whom I'd been speaking, just hours before, to a theater full of people in New York.

How can this be a coincidence? The same day I speak about her, the same day I said, "Rest after toil"—the same three words at the foot of her grave—this photo comes in the mail? These things make my head explode.

REST AFTER TOIL— the grave of Mabel Lavinia Rees (photo received September 21, 2015)

PARTING SHOTS:

1. "When you're a young actor," Rog said to me, "you dream about playing these great roles, and you think, *What will I do with them?* And then when you get to play them, you realize that you don't have to do anything at all. That's Shakespeare's recipe: take one great part, add one human being, stir, and stand well back. There's a great day when you realize that your Hamlet's arms will be never be any wider than your own, he will be exactly as tall as you, and he will sound just the way you sound. All Shakespeare seems to need is a human being, and you know what? We're all qualified."

2. "I never knew my father very well," Rog said to me. "He was a policeman—he was always off fighting crime; and, sadly for both of us, we hardly spoke during his lifetime. He was a tough man, and I always assumed, if he'd lived longer, he'd have had no interest at all in my passion for art and theater. Until, a few years after my father passed, my mother gave me a book called *Stories from Shakespeare*—small enough to put in your pocket—that my father carried with him every day when he was a schoolboy. How wrong I was about him. How much we could have discussed!"

3. I'm grateful beyond words to everyone who's written and been so kind. I feel I should be happier now, or settled at least. I'm like a vagrant snail, carrying this load of sadness on my back. It is hard to spot signs of recovery, hard to evaluate them. I ask myself, "Am I going in circles, or am I maybe on a spiral, moving back to the light, back to the living?" The first acute agony cannot last, but it comes back when you least expect it. It takes my breath away every time, and the tears flow, but it still feels preferable to the dread of what will replace it. Dread? What do I dread? Betrayal of Rog, of his memory, perpetrated by any recovery. Recovery, even an inch of it, feels like a betrayal. Passionately, I keep trying to find a way back to my sweetheart, but the only possible road, the road to life, leads away. Or does it? Is Rog really and truly gone, or can some part of him still be found?

It's an obscure, muddled process, a process with no logic and no timetable. I'm having a go at figuring out this loss, philosophically or emotionally. I'll take either at this point. But it's hard, heavy work. Sometimes I can't breathe for the weight of it. And what else can I do but write? So I have—even though what I feel doesn't give way easily to language. And what I've written is a play, since that is principally what I do.

It's called *Finding Roger*. Here's the final scene; a suggestion of how and where and why I might be lucky enough to find myself once more by his side.

Scene: Rick & Roger's Apartment—September 23, 2015

Rick

We hear the front door open and close.

Coo coo! Darling, I'm home!

Rick enters, wearing a jacket and tie and holding a plastic carrier bag from a market. He looks around.

Where are you? Where are you, Rog?

Nothing. He walks in a figure eight around the room. Crosses to the piano, plunks a few notes. Wipes his eyes.

Rog! Happy Anniversary, darling. And happy new year.

He reaches into the plastic bag and removes a glass containing a candle. It's a Yahrzeit memorial candle, lit on Yom Kippur—the holiest of Jewish holy days—to remember the dead.

I know I was supposed to light this last night, but I just—I couldn't bring myself to do it.

He places the candle next to a framed photograph of Roger.

I told Cantor Garfein at temple, and she said it'd be all right if I lit it tonight. I told her that would be even harder because it's September twenty-third, our anniversary.

(looks around for a match)

She looked at me like I was a little stupid, and then she said, "Only in the Jewish calendar does the holiday fall on the same day." Last year, Yom Kippur was October fourth. Next year, it'll be October twelfth.

(finds matches)

I said, "I know, dear. But this year, it's September twenty-third."

"God's little joke," she said.

(looks up)

Oh God—you're such a scamp.

Suddenly, the framed photo of Roger falls forward.

Are you kidding me?

(nothing)

Oh well. Happy Anniversary, darling.

He returns the photo to its standing position, then strikes a match and lights the memorial candle. As the flame comes to life, he recites:

"O, for a muse of fire that would ascend
The brightest heaven of invention,
A kingdom for a stage . . ."
> *But he chokes on the words.*

Oh, Rog . . .
> *From somewhere in the dark, he hears:*

Roger "A kingdom for a stage, princes to act,
And monarchs to behold the swelling scene."
> *The light changes. Roger is sitting in the armchair.*

Coo coo.
> *(Rick spins around . . .)*

Don't freak out. I can't stay very long.
> *(Rick stares at him, in shock . . .)*

You better sit down.

Rick Rog?

Roger Hallo, you.
> *Rick runs to him and hugs him.*

Rick Oh God Oh God Oh God. Thank you thank you thank you!

Roger I wasn't sure you'd be able to touch me.

Rick *(eyes filling with tears)* Where've you been, you bastard! What took you so long?

Roger It's only been a minute or two.

Rick Ten weeks! Ten weeks last Friday! Oh, my sweet baby—Where've you been?

Roger I was having Christmas dinner with Mum. And while she was plating a handsome slice of sticky toffee pudding, I thought, "I better check on Rick—he must be worried."

Rick *(tears streaming now)* But you love sticky toffee pudding.

Roger I know. I'm quite looking forward to it.

Rick I'm dreaming, aren't I? It's some sort of fever dream, because I've been fasting.

Roger Rick, you have to eat.

Rick I'm eating, believe me. Just not today. Today is Yom Kippur.

Roger But that's in the fall.

Rick It is the fall.

Roger Really? That's very curious.

Rick It's September twenty-third.

Roger That's our anniversary.

Rick That's right. Thirty-three years.

Roger You mean, Yom Kippur is on our anniversary this year?

Rick I know, right? Of all the days it could be, it just happens this year to be September twenty-third.

Roger You couldn't make that up, nobody would believe it.

Rick Nobody would believe you sitting here, either.

Roger God's little joke, I suppose.

Rick That's what Cantor Garfein said.

Roger Oh, how is lovely Cantor Garfein?

Rick She was in very good voice today. Thrilling, actually.

Roger Did she sing "L'dor V'ador"?

Rick Yes. I cried all the way through it. More than when she sang it at your funeral.

Roger She sang it then, too?

Rick Weren't you there?

Roger I told you, I've been with Mum.

> *Rick moves away, shaking his head. Then:*

Rick I'm losing my mind. That's it, isn't it?

Roger If you don't know how this works, Dickens explains it beautifully in *Tale of Two Cities.*

> *(then)*

You did read *Tale of Two Cities.*

Rick It's been a while.

Roger *(a gentle character voice)* "Do you think that it will seem long to me, while I wait for you in the better land where I trust both you and I will be mercifully reunited one day?"

> *(then, in a different voice)*

"It cannot seem long, my darling. There is no Time in Heaven, and no trouble there, either."

Rick So you've memorized all of Dickens now?

Roger Apparently.

Rick How?

Roger Science doesn't have all the answers. Anyway, the gist of it is—

Rick The gist of it is: Time is a wavy curtain.

Roger That's right. For you, it's been ten weeks. For me, it's been a pleasant afternoon with Mum.

Rick   Can you stay? Can you stay here with me now?

Roger Tell me about this candle again. What's it called?

Rick   Yahrzeit. Memorial candles. This is your first one. Today of all days. How am I supposed to light your first Yahrzeit on the anniversary of our first kiss?

Roger Darling, you need to be a bit more jolly.

Rick   But I don't feel jolly! I feel despair! I ache . . .
           (poking himself in the chest)
           In here. How do I live out the days, Rog? I don't know how . . .

Roger You work.

Rick   I can't work! I can't put two words together! I've lost my muse.

Roger You still have our friends.

Rick   They don't want me, they want you!

Roger Don't be a prat. They love you, talk to them.

Rick   It doesn't help! It makes me nuts, everyone telling me to move on. How'm I supposed to move on without my arms and my legs?

Roger It's just a metaphor, Rick.

Rick   I know it's a metaphor, Roger! But it hurts. It hurts in my heart. I just want to be with you!

Roger I know, darling, but not yet. I can see you, as an old man, weeping for me on the anniversary of this day. And after that, further on, I see us both, both our courses run at last, sitting side by side high on a hill, each of us held sacred in the other's heart. But not yet.

Rick   Yeah, but what'm I supposed to do in the meantime?

Roger You're all that's left of me now. You have a responsibility.

Rick   To do what?

Roger To bloody well keep at it!

Rick   I don't know how!

Roger You need to get out of this apartment, for starters.

Rick   What's the point? Where does the bereft person dwell, except in his grief?

Roger Well, that's a real toe-tapper, isn't it? I want you to be in the world, and of the world—not off to the side, watching.

Rick   Doesn't matter where I go, I'm just going in circles. Around and around and around, asking, where are you, where are you?

Roger You've been looking in the wrong place.

Rick But you're here, we're home. Can't we just stay like this? It's enough; it's perfect.

Roger Perfection is a moving point.

Rick *(sniffling)* What is that, like a fortune cookie?

Roger I think it's why I'm happy. Why I've always been able to be happy.

Rick You would've been much happier if we never met.

Roger Bollocks.

Rick You would've been a huge star. It was all happening for you. "It's a privilege to see Roger Rees at this flowering of his skills," they said.

Roger I don't remember that.

Rick Because you're the world's most modest person. You would've stayed in England and had a great career, you would've been Sir Roger probably . . . and you gave it all up.

Roger But I got you.

Rick Yeah, a crazy person with anger issues.

Roger *My* crazy person. I think I did pretty well out of it.

Rick Then stay! Five more minutes! I don't want it to end!

Roger It doesn't end. We'll always celebrate September twenty-third.
>   *(kisses him)*
> Always, always, always, always, always.
>   *(kisses him again)*
> But I can't stay.
>   *He rises to leave.*

Rick *(desperate)* No! We can't be parted, we only just got back together!

Roger You used to think that was very romantic. Warriors of love— parting and meeting and parting and meeting . . . By the way, have you seen any good plays lately?

Rick What?

Roger Have you seen any good plays lately? A good old well-made play might be just the ticket.

Rick I can't be in a theater, Rog. It's too hard.

Roger I'm sorry, I thought you said you've been looking for me?

Rick Every day. At the dog run, in Shakespeare's Garden. I tried the museum, I waited by the Delacroix, like that time when I couldn't find you and—

Roger *(interrupting)* Funny, you haven't looked for me in a theater. It's the place I'd have gone first of all.

Rick Wait—

Roger The place where we first met. Where we feel most alive. We could spend a few hours together, just the way we started.

Rick *(smacks his head)* Rick, you idiot!

Roger *(riding over)* Yes, there'll be parting. But there'll be wonderful, thrilling, glorious reunions, too.

Rick In a theater? That's where you'll be?

Roger Every time you go.

Rick Can you do that? Just show up?

      Roger plunks a few notes on the piano and sings:

Roger THOUGH I'M CERTAIN
THAT THIS HEART OF MINE
HASN'T A GHOST OF A CHANCE—
      (stops)
A bit on the nose, but you get the idea—
      (sings)
YOU GO TO MY HEAD . . .

Rick God, how did I not think of this!
      He hugs Roger close.

Roger You've had kind of a lot on your mind.

Rick Warriors of love, absolutely, back in the saddle!
      (abruptly, pulling back)
And I'll be able to find you?

Roger I imagine so. The theater's been very good to us.
      They kiss.
Always liked the way our lips fit together.
      Rick holds on to Roger for dear life.

Rick Don't make me let you go. I don't want to get used to you not being here. I don't want to forget to miss you.

Roger Then write, darling. Write me down and I'll last forever.

Rick I can't!

Roger You have to. Write the world you want to live in. And that's where I'll be. Happy Anniversary, darling.
      He pulls himself free and turns toward the darkness. But Rick can't let him disappear.

Rick ROG!

> *Roger turns back.*

I'm your chap.

Roger *(smiles)* I know. Aren't we lucky?

> *Roger waves and disappears.*
> *The memorial candle is still lit, flickering in the darkness.*
> *Rick shakes his head . . . what just happened?*
> *But there's something he feels the need to do, for the first time in a long time.*
> *He goes to his desk, opens his computer . . .*
> *The screen comes on, illuminating Rick's face.*
> *He looks behind him—quite alone—turns back, thinks for a moment . . .*
> *. . . and begins to write.*

Curtain

REMEMBERING ROGER

THOMAS SCHUMACHER /
Introduction at Roger's Memorial

Our beloved Roger Rees, rhymes with "can of peas." Like most of you, I fell in love with Roger on the stage and screen, both large and small, but I actually met Rog right back there, house right, behind the last row, in this very theater some eighteen years ago. And while Rog didn't perform on this stage (although the inaugural production here in 1904 was *A Midsummer Night's Dream*), he was very much a part of the Disney theatrical family.

First of course by marriage, to one of the pillars of our company, the *sine qua non* of Disney theatricals, Rick Elice. Rick first brought Roger into our circle, and then Roger took his own very prominent place as the director, with Alex Timbers, of our much beloved *Peter and the Starcatcher.* That production was given birth at my breakfast table at our home in the country, on one of the many weekends Roger and Rick visited—when I asked Roger if he thought there was a way of theatricalizing the beautiful novel by Dave Barry and Ridley Pearson.

Roger was a man of extraordinary generosity of spirit. Though a fancy classical actor to the public, he was always willing to don a funny hat or worse at one of our "Christmas Spectaculars" at home, narrate the odd puppet show on a moment's notice, or whip out a sonnet at a picnic or on one of the many stages we visited in Italy. He loved sharing himself, and his passions, and I defy anyone to not have been transported by him. Today we celebrate what he meant to us in both the public and the personal realms. We'll hear from some friends in person and by proxy and we will remember together what a joy Roger was to behold.

Remembering Roger:

I'll always remember what Andre Bishop said when we cast Roger in *A Man of No Importance*: "Roger is perfect for the part. He embodies the essence of a good man." A good man, not to mention a gent, a clown, a bravura actor, an extremely kind person, a leader, an organizer, a bold spirit, a dear heart, a self-effacing charmer, a wit, and a *mensch*. I wish I had known him longer, done more shows with him, had more dinners with him. I think about *A Man of No Importance* now as the show where my 1981 crush on Roger Rees solidified into worship. His spirit must have entered my pen and made me write lyrics that seem, now, to be all about him:

For life is clearly something that I can't rehearse.
It's dangerous and beautiful and free as verse.
And rather than avoid it, it's high time I stood in its way . . .
Welcome to the world, I am in the world.
That should be enough, and that's all I have to say.

— **Lynn Ahrens, lyricist**

Yesterday, I happened to hear "The Streets of Dublin" playing somewhere and was reminded of that time and your remarkable, galvanizing performance. Thank you for that, Rog.

—**Joe Mantello, director**

Here at the Royal Shakespeare Company, Roger will be lovingly remembered for the rest of our lives. He embodied everything the RSC is about, graduating through the ranks, year after year, until he was playing Hamlet, and proving that as well as possessing an uncanny comic flare, he could also be a charismatic musical performer, when he played opposite Judi Dench in one of the RSC's biggest hits, the musical *Comedy of Errors*. *Nicholas Nickleby*, of course, was something else again. Roger was the leader—of the company, of the show, of believing in the impossible. The iconic poster for that show pictures Roger punching the air, in determination, in defiance, in unquenchable courage, and in triumph. Yes, he was a wonderfully original actor, but above all, he was a mighty spirit who lifted up everyone around him.

—**Greg Doran, artistic director,
Royal Shakespeare Company**

The light of Roger will never dim in our lives. It will shine like he did—onstage and in life. Roger was always and will forever be a beacon. I cannot help but smile at the very thought of him—his joyfulness, his antic humor, his slyness, and his embrace. I bless and cherish our friendship.

—**Michael Ritchie, artistic director,
Los Angeles' Center Theatre Group**

Whatever Roger was engaged in—playing a part in a play or scheming about fun and games backstage or unveiling the little cakes he had bought for our intermission snack during *Indiscretions*, or chatting to kids at a Q & A, or simply walking onto the stage for his Shakespeare show—he would shine. He really would. He was a very special, divinely sexy man whose love and energy were all-embracing, a light in everyone's life.

—**Kathleen Turner, actor**

Roger's great qualities were a tremendous energy, his total commitment to the language, and an ability to turn on a sixpence from tragedy to comedy and back again. This is something only very good actors can do. And backstage, there is nobody better, more joyful, or more fun. Nobody.

—**Jane Lapotaire, actor**

Sinead and I were so sad to hear of the terrible news of Roger's departure from our lives. Although since his emigration to America for the green pastures of love, we rarely saw him (the last time, at that Irish restaurant on, I think, Fifty-Third Street). We always enjoyed seeing his work, and loved him powerfully indeed.

—**Jeremy Irons, actor**

This is just to hold your hands across the sea in celebration of the essential Roger, a blessing to all who knew him and a fine example of what it is to be a man. I had such wonderful years working with him and loving him and being in his light. The times with Rog in *The Real Thing* and *Hapgood* are crystal clear and utterly precious.

—**Felicity Kendal, actor**

What a beautiful man—in body and spirit! His goodness shone out of him. But somebody should mention his face. I don't think Roger had a bad-looking day in his life. With Love.

—**Sir Tom Stoppard, playwright**

Roger changed the trajectory of my life. I was his dresser on *The Red Shoes*, though, as these things sometimes turn out, not for long. Immediately after that, Roger called Victor Garber and told him to hire me. If he hadn't done that, I really don't know where I would've ended up; probably slinging hash in some low-down, dirty dinner theater in the Midwest. But no. Thanks to Roger, I'm making a career in the New York theater—in the wings, mind you—but a real career, where I have thrived, because of Roger and his kindness all those years ago.

—**Joe Hickey, crew**

Every now and then, a couple of times in one's adult life if you're lucky—you get to meet someone as gifted and deep-souled and subtle and wonderful as Roger. Our days together filming last summer were so joyous for all of us; just to be with him and to watch and marvel as he coaxed great power and feeling out of words and moments, often where you would least expect to find them. We live with Roger's remarkable performance in *The Pilgrims*—his final performance on film—day in and day out in our editing room. It's a spectacular performance. What a rare person Roger was. He made our film soar.

—**Ric Burns, Steeplechase Films**

Roger was a guest teacher in my Shakespeare class at Fordham and, in one single day, he literally changed my life. I've called on so many lessons from that class ever since. From my approach to Shakespeare (very modern, very fast, kind of a balance between Brando and Gielgud) to how I hope to approach life with great zest and joy, Roger's class was a complete education unto itself. My friends from that class still volley lines of "Shall I compare thee to a summer's day" back and forth. So brilliant. Roger totally knew the secret of life. And he gave every one of us a joyous and transformative experience.

—**Jeffrey Glaser, former student**

I was onstage with Roger for every single performance of *Nicholas Nickleby* at the RSC in the UK and New York. He was just wonderful to watch every time, such brilliant acting, such charisma, 100 percent energy and commitment at every performance, which on occasion left him completely exhausted after the show. He was incredibly kind, but with that distinctive wit and humor that always hit the nail on the head. He led our company brilliantly, but was never grand or above anybody else. He was unique and wonderful and, like everyone else, I truly, truly loved him.

—**Janet Dale, actor**

When I first met Roger, over fifty years ago, he wasn't an actor and I wasn't a director. He was a student at the Slade School of Art (I still have one of his designs on my walls), who came to be an extra in a Greek tragedy at the Hampstead Theatre, where I was general manager. We made each other laugh, a very good starting point for any relationship, and when he went to the

Pitlochry Theatre for a year to learn his trade, we corresponded regularly—people still wrote letters back then. He took a break from the RSC in 1972 and joined me at Cambridge, where we did six plays over nine months, my first ensemble company, from which we emerged firmer friends and with a great mutual respect. We did six plays in nine months; Brecht, Ionesco, and Shakespeare. But Rog and Zoë Wanamaker in Rattigan's *French Without Tears*—that was the surprise hit. Four years later, when he was back at the RSC, it was a great thrill when Trevor Nunn and the company of *The Three Sisters* chose my translation for their hugely successful production, in which Rog was an unforgettable Tusenbach. I remember so many of his performances—the Young Shepherd in *Winter's Tale*, Witwood in *Way of the World*, Semyon in *The Suicide*, Henry in *The Real Thing*, Kerner in *Hapgood*, Posthumus in *Cymbeline*.

Then came *Nicholas Nickleby* and Rick Elice. Rog went to live in America and I moved to Australia to join *my* life partner. So we saw less of each other. But distance couldn't really separate Roger and me. In 1998, I was asked to direct him and Dana Ivey in *The Uneasy Chair* for Playwrights' Horizons. To work with two such actors in a new play in New York in early autumn was like being given a lot of presents all at once and I would walk down Broadway every day, pinching myself to make sure I wasn't dreaming. Roger was funny, he was elusive—he never liked being pinned down—he was a loving friend, he gave wonderful presents.

Speaking of presents, Rog loved the off-the-wall variety. When he went to Tokyo with the RSC, there was an earthquake. The audience fled while the actors continued playing *Othello*. Rog memorialized that shaky matinee by sending me a Japanese poster advertising the before-and-after benefits of laxatives. Thinking of our fifty years of friendship, Joe Gargery, the blacksmith in *Great Expectations*, comes to mind: "*What larks, old chap.*"

Dear Rog, what larks indeed.

—Richard Cottrell, director

Beautiful artist, beautiful actor, beautiful man. Visionary, too. When he was running the Bristol Old Vic in the 1980s, he formed a multiracial acting company before it was the trendy thing to do. That really rocked the town, I can tell you. Rog had an unshakable belief in the power of the ensemble, and he made sure everyone felt important, including the audience. Including me. He made me feel silly, too. And I loved him for it.

—**Zoë Wanamaker, actor**

It cannot be that the honest, trustworthy, funny, kind, open man who literally carried me through eighteen months of my life has gone. Playing Nicholas and Smike, two strangers who turned out to be cousins, cemented a deep bond in us, even when an ocean kept us at distance with only sporadic meetings, quick catch-up gossip, and jokes. Distance has never, ever meant out of mind as far as Roger's been concerned. Frankly, I have lost family members that have not affected me as much. The light of love and friendship is real, Roger. It burns bright and always will.

—**David Threlfall, actor**

At the height of his *Nickleby* fame, I idiotically told Roger he wouldn't fulfill his potential until he could develop "repose." What a ridiculous assertion—like telling Jackson Pollock he would never get anywhere until he learnt to control paint. One moment with Rog, his simple poignancy would have us spellbound; seconds later, he'd have us roaring with laughter. This is true onstage, or walking with him through the Metropolitan Museum of Art. Which on several occasions, created quite a stir at the Metropolitan Museum of Art.

—**Edward Petherbridge, actor/writer**

Roger Rees was the single most stunning creature this earth has ever amounted to, and simply the sight of him always brought the broadest of smiles to my face.

—**Sir Ian McKellen, actor/writer**

Rog was without doubt one of the very best people I have ever known. Such a good man.

—**Dame Judi Dench, actor**

Some people claim it was Eleanor Roosevelt, but I think it was a Welsh rugby player who said, "Many people walk in and out of your life, but only true friends leave footprints in your heart." That was Roger Rees.

—**Sir Patrick Stewart, actor**

In 1996, I first saw Roger striding through the lobby of the apartment building where we both live. I thought that he looked forbidding. I mentioned this to a friend and she said, "You couldn't be more mistaken." How right she was. Roger was a dear, warm, wonderfully talented man.

—**Sheldon Harnick, lyricist**

Roger my dearest darling—I know you're as popular in heaven as Lady Diana Cooper, but if you'd enjoy the company of a fairly fresh great lady of the stage for a laugh or two, do come back and visit anytime. With love.

—**Charles Busch, actor/writer**

You carried me on your shoulders in *Romeo and Juliet* and pulled a mouse out of your Restoration wig and handed it to me in *The Way of the World*. I remember our two solo Shakespeare shows; the calls we made from one theater to another during intermissions; the book about Russia you illustrated for me (your fee—a bottle of tequila). And you had this gift for just turning up. I thought you were in New York, and there you'd be, out of the blue, at a matinee at Chichester. When I saw *Peter and the Starcatcher*, we beamed at each other in a sort of silent glee at the way our lives had turned out. You burned so bright, and like everyone here, I feel a part of me has dropped off. I shall love you, my friend, till the day I go myself.

—**Michael Pennington, actor/writer**

I knew Roger at the RSC when I stage-managed there in the late sixties and early seventies. Rog came up in the ranks while Ian Richardson, Ian McKellen, Pat Stewart, and Ben Kingsley were getting most of the attention. Frankly, they could all be handfuls. But not Rog. Rog was special. He was also beautiful. You wouldn't ordinarily use that word for a man, but that's what he was. So much so that on the first night of *Merry Wives of Windsor*, Ian Richardson turned to Roger and instructed him thus, "Go back to your dressing room right now and take off your jockstrap. They're going to be queuing for you at the stage door, Rog. They're going to be lining up for you right the way down to London."

—**Roger Gregory, stage manager**

Mercurial, mystical, mischievous, magical, magnificent Rog. Always an inspiration. Sensitive, witty, smart, and funny; such a very funny guy. A beautiful man, a beautiful friend, Roger Rees.

—**Sara Kestelman, actor**

This extraordinarily GOOD GUY. This paragon of talent and kindness. How can Roger be gone? Rick, you were loved by THE BEST.

—**Tommy Tune, actor/director/choreographer**

Everybody loved Roger, everybody admired him; everybody was a little bit in love with him. He was a great person and a great artist. I well remember having dinner with Rick years ago, when he told me how he first met Roger and set his cap for him. Look at the wonderfully long and happy marriage that ensued.

—**Andre Bishop, artistic director, Lincoln Center Theater**

Giving Roger his first directing job in America—*Red Memories* at New York Stage and Film—was, and is, one of the things I am most proud of in my career. His fierce intelligence, his sense of fun, and his naughty impishness made for a great experience. Roger and Rick have been a beacon of stability in a community where that isn't always the case. I always looked to the two of them as role models.

—**Peter Manning, former artistic director, New York Stage and Film**

Throughout all the years of crazy New York living, I've met maybe five couples who've made me think, "That's it, that's the real thing. They love each other absolutely." Roger and Rick were like that. A romance for the ages.

—**Susan Morrison, *The New Yorker* magazine**

I believe I was the first to dub Roger and Rick "R&R," just after I produced *The Real Thing* in 1982. Fond memories of that duo, so new to each other back then, yet somehow already the happiest of couples, sustain me now.

—**Sir Michael Codron, producer**

Some of my greatest experiences in theater have been with Roger. What a great man of the theater he was. But what most resonates for me is the great love story of Roger and Rick. They were partners in the truest sense of the word, and I have learned so much about love from them. They taught me that our greatest capacity as human beings is our ability to love. The joy that radiated from them was so special and they shared it with all of us.

—**Florie Seery, general manager, Manhattan Theatre Club**

It was bliss seeing Roger and Rick together. The happiness on their faces, the way they took care of each other would remind me that love between two people was possible—and wonderful.

—**Jorge Vargas, artist**

Thank you for the dashingly beautiful, endlessly gracious, tremendously kind, and alarmingly talented Roger Rees. The amazing life that Roger and Rick had together and their astonishing relationship and marriage should continue on and on.

—**Kathleen Marshall, director/choreographer**

I'd like to tell you all what a wonderful experience it was to get to know Roger when we produced his one-man show in London three years ago. I'm so happy to have worked with a true gentleman of the theater; gloriously skilled, smart as anything, screamingly funny, and deeply kind. It doesn't get better than that, and I'm so proud and grateful to have gotten to know Rog and Rick together as friends. My spirits are lifted by that.

— **Nick Frankfort, producer**

I feel blessed to know Roger. I use the present tense because even though he is physically not here, I truly believe his spirit and his legacy live on, especially through Rick and the beautiful stories he shares about their life together. Roger was exceptional and the two of them together were truly breathtaking.

—**Cantor Rebecca Garfein,
Congregation Rodeph Sholom**

I knew Roger when we were teenagers. We both attended St. Mark's Church, Battersea Rise in South London. We helped with outings for the younger children, including Roger's crazy brother, Andrew. We did the crossword together, talked endlessly about art and literature. Roger introduced me to Bannister Fletcher's book on architecture, which I have to this day. He was very lovable even then; a good man even though he was not much more than a boy. We were only sixteen or seventeen, but I think it's fair to say we were sort of girlfriend and boyfriend. Sorry, Rick.

—**Mary Hoffman, friend**

Roger's passing has helped me to further appreciate two men whom I did not believe it possible to appreciate further. Working with Roger and Rick on *Double Double* at Williamstown is one of my fondest memories in the theater. I'll never forget the meal they just "threw together" on closing night for Jennifer Van Dyck and her husband, and me, my wife, and kids. Roger and Rick kept claiming that they had no idea what they were doing, but the results were sumptuous and utterly perfect. And I started to think that maybe that was the process for everything they did together. "No clue, you?" "None whatsoever." "Great! Let's get to work!"

—**Matt Letscher, actor**

Dear Rick: I remember sitting with Rog in your beautiful home several months ago. We were directly across the room from you. As a lull came in our conversation, Roger gently shifted his focus and began staring across at you. The sweetness in his look was something I couldn't take my eyes from. And as he looked, I remember him saying so softly, like no one could hear, "Isn't he wonderful? God, I'm so lucky. And he's all mine . . . I'll tell him someday. I'll tell him." It was one of those moments that showed me, that reminded me, what true love is. And how it is never gone. How Roger must be staring at you from Heaven right now, guiding your hand, never leaving your side.

—**George Abud, actor**

Dear Rog: You may be gone, but I thought I'd write and tell you how glad I am that we've been friends. When we were doing all those charity benefits in LA, you were the one that had all the ideas, but you always made me feel that I was fabulously inventive and clever, too. The truth was that you were the brilliant one, and were kind enough to shine your light on me. We had a few laughs though, didn't we? Doing *Merry Wives* for you was a highlight in a long career for me. I had such a wonderful time working with you, and it was such a happy company of actors. We'd have done anything for you, Rog. If you'd asked us to say our lines dangling from an elastic band from the rafters, we'd have gladly complied. Colossal amounts of love, dear friend.

—**Jane Carr, actor**

I met Roger when I was working at the Valadon Hotel in 1989 near the Sunset Strip. Roger had just joined the cast of *Cheers*, and was staying at the hotel until he and Rick could find a house to rent. I was a struggling actor trying to make ends meet. Roger always talked to me about plays and theater, and I want to tell you about a noble gesture he did for me that I remember to this day. He drove a long distance by himself on a Saturday night to attend a play I appeared in—*Hedda Gabler*—in which I portrayed George Tesman, Hedda's husband. After the performance, Roger presented me with a magnificent gift: a biography of Laurence Olivier, autographed by the entire cast of *Cheers*. He was a supremely kindred spirit with a heart as big as all the theaters in London—and as kind as anyone I've ever met. We have a word in Yiddish: mensch—that's a man with total class. Roger is the quintessential embodiment of that word.

—**Howard Liebgot, actor**

The first time I met Roger was at an audition for *Anything Goes*, which Rog was directing at Williamstown. Tara Rubin Casting contacted me at the Broadway Dance Center, where I'm on the faculty, asking me to recommend a really good middle-aged tap dancer. "Well," I said, "it sounds like you're looking for me!" I got an appointment; it was just one other lady and me. And I got the job. It was one of the best experiences of my life. I won't lie. I may have fallen a little bit in love with him. Is there anyone who didn't? A year ago, he came to my class at the Broadway Dance Center to brush up his tap skills for a new role. We only got to tap together a few times before he got sick. He was such a prize student—so curious and tenacious. The last time I saw him was in *The Visit* in May. I told him to stay in touch and he looked me in the eye and said, "I promise." I believe he will live up to that promise. He was magnetic, he was charming, and so very, very special. Fred Ebb said it best in *The Visit*: "He must have been something." He certainly was.

—**Crystal Chapman, dancer/instructor**

Dear Roger. Kind, generous of spirit, present in every moment. I loved the way you let others step forward and shine, while you held space for them to do so. And, oh, how I loved watching you act. Never a lone star, but always sharing the spotlight, both on- and offstage. So much to learn from your beautiful way of being. And then there were the personal moments. Holiday dinners, picnics, and openings. Roger, the friend, warm and loving, a curious listener. Happy to indulge us with a Shakespeare sonnet or a few pages of Dickens. Oh, how special we all felt. That's it. You made me feel special. How did you inhabit and hold such a range of qualities? It was such a gift to see you in that tender space a few days before you passed. Beautiful you, in your makeshift bedroom, sitting there so gently. Thank you for being so beautifully in the world, for elevating all of us by your presence. I wish for your next adventure to be filled with great joy and love. I have no doubt it is.

—**Michele Steckler, producer**

The late, very great Roger Rees left an indelible mark on me personally and professionally beginning with our time together in *Peter and the Starcatcher*. I have a catalog of memories of him in greenrooms, stage doors, rehearsal halls, dressing rooms, and on stages around the country. We'd often talk about Shakespeare, and he'd ask me about my Hamlet. ("What will he be like?") He seemed to always be eating almonds, which I regarded as some magical elixir that added years, youthfulness, and soulfulness to one's life. I immediately adopted the habit myself, and, to this day, continue chomping on them daily. His head of hair is something I aspire to, as well. But that goes without saying. He made life seem infinite, that aging was something that didn't have to happen if you didn't want it to. He was living proof that a life in theater could, in fact, amount to a life well lived. He believed that your imagination could change the world. I thought and hoped that he would live forever. But, of course: "We change. We grow up. It always happens. Nothing is forever. That's the rule. Everything ends." And one more line from Rick's script that rings so true: "It's supposed to hurt. That's how you know it meant something." It meant something, Rog. And God, it hurts.

—**Carl Howell, actor**

In my *Starcatcher* audition, Roger strode right up to me, grasped my hand, and said to this nobody: "How do I know you? I must know you." All the while, looking straight through me, it felt, to someplace deep. I stammered something incoherent and recollect little of what followed. I know how blessed I am to have had so much time with Roger. Working with him was a yearlong master class with a true master. An astonishingly witty, bright, soulful, devastatingly handsome master. His memory is a blessing and it forever will be.

—**Megan Stern, actor**

Roger was inspirational. He had the perpetual boyishness and mischief of a Peter Pan, extraordinary wit combined with a gift for self-satire, and dauntless optimism. All these ingredients went into his acting and his directing, and gave him an aura of rare, generous-spirited humanity. He was always superb at being just "one of the gang," while equally deft at leading by example, leading by commitment. All this was sublimated in his Nicholas Nickleby, the giant success of which changed his life. I spent a magical evening with Roger and Rick in New York only a few months ago. Rog talked of his illness—with that same wit, self-satire, and optimism . . . and once again, to be in his presence was inspirational. Then we hugged. And neither of us could let go. From the moment I met him forty-eight years ago, Rog has been not just a vital gigantic presence in my professional career, but in my life.

I think of him always in terms of family, as somebody without whose presence my life would be a lesser, smaller, darker thing. My house has many pictures of him. I will continue to gaze on those images and get more of his inspiration, more of his humanity, more of his goodness, and courage and love.

—**Sir Trevor Nunn, director**

Dear Rick, Roger's company and the very thought of Roger have always made me happy. And I have never thought of him without thinking of you. His easy, generous joy in finding you was so infectious and inspiring, and the certainty of your togetherness from the moment I first saw you together back in Stratford in '84 was so tangible and real and right. The greatest part of being in NY last summer was seeing you both and feeling that, between Roger and me, this meeting was very, very meaningful. I have many thank-yous to make in my life, but one of the deepest was to Roger that night, to say how utterly inspiring his natural artistry and humanity were to me. I was blessed to be around him and laugh with him, and notice, so very clearly, that here was a rare and great spirit. Of course you are brokenhearted. But how much he loved you. How much. And how profoundly grateful he was for the life you created together, how gloriously happy. I send you love, love, love, love, love.

—**Sir Kenneth Branagh, actor/writer/director**

Yesterday, *Waiting for Godot* played Khayelitsha, the largest township here in Cape Town, South Africa. Samuel Beckett would have been proud. We played in a gymnasium on a temporary stage. The first play ever performed in a township. No sets, no lights, just us. We were watched by young children, and men and women who'd scraped by somehow and survived the hellish days of District Six in Soweto. One million people live in this vast shantytown. Row after row of corrugated tin huts with no electricity other than what can be thieved from the power lines high overhead and dangerously transmitted down to these metal homes on what? Coat hangers. Homes? Well, they have to pay extra for windows and doors, and many can't. Sheep's heads are cooking away to welcome home busloads of workers—the city's janitors and maids. We went into several homes, welcomed by old Go-Go's, or grandmothers, in a community where the old people are revered. The children look up at you with eyes full of joy, and smiles fill their faces.

And then we performed the play, enhanced by birds on the wing through the gymnasium roof, babies howling, rapt, sepulchral silences, then circus-like booms of uproarious laughter—the whole tragicomedy of it was there, and it was one of the best experiences of my life.

Aren't we lucky?

—Roger Rees, South Africa, August 2010

ROGER REES, A RESUME

ROGER REES was born in Aberystwyth, Wales, United Kingdom, on May 5, 1944, and grew up in South London. He wanted to be an artist. He was at a pretty rough school, and the only thing he was good at—and the thing that saved him—was art. He was accepted into the prestigious Camberwell College of Art and studied to be a painter. He sketched so well that he was accepted into the Slade School of Fine Art, one of the world's preeminent art schools.

When his father died, Roger left the Slade and painted scenery to support his mother and his brother. He was painting scenery at Wimbledon Theatre when Arthur Lane, that theater's actor/manager, needed a young man to be in a play—and suddenly Roger became an actor. He played the lead, and he wasn't nervous. He learned to be nervous later. Meanwhile, he appeared in Agatha Christie plays, *A Christmas Carol* (which began his lifelong passion for Dickens), seasonal pantomimes, even as the front half of a dancing cow.

In 1966, he auditioned for the Royal Shakespeare Company and was sent away because his voice wasn't very good. He moved north to Scotland, and became a stage manager at the Pitlochry Theatre Festival. One of the young actors in the troupe fell ill and Roger replaced him onstage, playing parts like Yasha, the manservant, in *The Cherry Orchard*—which began his lifelong passion for Chekhov.

A year later he auditioned again for the RSC and was accepted. His first role was as a nonspeaking hunstman in *The Taming of the Shrew*—thus beginning his lifelong passion for Shakespeare. He worked his way up over the course of twenty-two years with the company, playing roles including Graziano in *Merchant of Venice*, Roderigo in *Othello*, Aguecheek in *Twelfth Night*, and eventually became one of Trevor Nunn's leading actors—playing Antipholus in *The Comedy of Errors*,

Semyon in *The Suicide*, Berowne in *Love's Labour's Lost*, and Hamlet. His most famous role for the RSC is the title role he created in *The Life and Adventures of Nicholas Nickleby*.

Roger won the Olivier Award in London, the Tony Award in New York, plus an Emmy nomination for Best Actor for the role of Nicholas Nickleby. Roger remained an associate artist of the Royal Shakespeare Company for the rest of his life.

In London, Roger created the starring roles of Henry and Kerner, both opposite Felicity Kendal, in Tom Stoppard's *The Real Thing* and *Hapgood*, and played opposite Jane Lapotaire in his own thriller, *Double Double*, which was coauthored with Rick Elice.

In 2010, Roger returned to London to play Vladimir opposite Ian McKellen's Estragon in the critically acclaimed production of *Waiting for Godot* at the Theatre Royal, Haymarket. The production toured throughout Australia, New Zealand, and South Africa.

On and off-Broadway, Roger Rees appeared in *London Assurance* with Donald Sinden; *Nicholas Nickleby*; *Indiscretions* with Kathleen Turner, Eileen Atkins, Cynthia Nixon, and Jude Law (Tony, Drama Desk nominations); John Robin Baitz's *The End of the Day* (Obie Award); *Uncle Vanya* with Derek Jacobi and Laura Linney; *The Uneasy Chair* with Dana Ivey; *The Rehearsal* with David Threlfall and Frances Conroy; *The Misanthrope* opposite Uma Thurman; the world premiere of the Terrence McNally/Lynn Ahrens/Stephen Flaherty musical, *A Man of No Importance* with Faith Prince, Steven Pasquale, and Sally Murphy; as Gomez opposite the Morticias of Bebe Neuwirth and Brooke Shields in *The Addams Family*; and as Arthur Winslow in *The Winslow Boy* with Mary Elizabeth Mastrantonio and Alessandro Nivola.

Some of his films are *The Ebony Tower* (opposite Laurence Olivier), Mel Brooks's *Robin Hood: Men in Tights*, Bob Fosse's *Star 80*, Julie Taymor's *Frida*, Christopher Nolan's *The Prestige*, Peter Greenaway's *A Life in Suitcases*, and Richard Squires's *Crazy Like a Fox*, opposite Mary McDonnell.

Known to television audiences as Lord John Marbury on *The West Wing* and Robin Colcord on *Cheers*, Roger also played Dr. Colin Marlow in *Grey's Anatomy* and has appeared in *Oz, My So-Called Life, MANTIS, Warehouse 13, The Good Wife, Elementary*, and such television movies as *The Crossing, Double Platinum, Titanic*, and *Liberty*. On Thanksgiving 2015, he was seen on PBS in his final film role in Ric Burns's documentary, *The Pilgrims*.

From 1986–88, Roger served as associate artistic director of the Bristol Old Vic where he directed, among others, *Julius Caesar, Turkey Time*, and *John Bull*.

In America, Roger directed *Red Memories* (New York Stage and Film); *Mud, River Stone* (Playwrights Horizons); *The Merry Wives of Windsor*; *Love's Labour's Lost* and *Dog and Pony* (Old Globe); *Arms and the Man* (Roundabout); and an episode of HBO's *Oz*. Roger, for three very happy years (2005–2007), was the artistic director of the Williamstown Theatre Festival, where he directed *The Rivals*, Robbie Baitz's *The Film Society*, Simon Grey's *The Late Middle Classes*, Cole Porter's *Anything Goes, Herringbone* (starring B. D. Wong), and *Double Double* (with Matt Letscher and Jennifer Van Dyck). He also directed *The Taming of the Shrew*, in which he played Petruchio opposite Bebe Neuwirth's Katherine.

With the much-loved Collegiate Chorale (now Master Voices) at Lincoln Center, Roger directed Scott Joplin's *Treemonisha*, Philip Glass's *Juniper Tree*, George Gershwin's *White House Cantata*, and Kurt Weill's *Firebrand of Florence*. He conceived and directed *Here Lies Jenny* starring Bebe Neuwirth, with choreography by Ann Reinking, which ran successfully in New York and San Francisco.

In 2011, Roger and Alex Timbers teamed to direct *Peter and the Starcatcher* by Rick Elice, which is based on the novel by Dave Barry and Ridley Pearson, at the New York Theatre Workshop. They won the Obie Award for Outstanding Direction. In 2012, the play opened on Broadway, garnering more Tony nominations (nine) than any new American play in the history of the Tony Awards, including one for Best Direction of a Play. The production won five awards. Their production played on and off-Broadway for two years and enjoyed a successful national tour starting in 2013.

A year after the premiere of *Starcatcher*, in the fall of 2012, Roger took his one-man show, *What You Will*—devoted to his life and adventures with William Shakespeare—to London's West End. The show, which Roger toured throughout the United States, premiered in 2006 at the Folger Shakespeare Theatre in Washington, DC. In the summer of 2014, Roger starred opposite Chita Rivera in the Terrence McNally/John Kander/Fred Ebb musical *The Visit*, directed by John Doyle and choreographed by Graciela Daniele. On April 23, 2015, *The Visit* opened on Broadway. It was Roger's last show.

On November 16, 2015, Roger was posthumously inducted into The American Theater Hall of Fame.

In 1982, Roger met Rick Elice. They were together as a couple ever since, and married legally in 2011.

ACKNOWLEDGMENTS

I would like to express my gratitude and appreciation, once more, to Nancy Coyne, who told me to write, and to Marshall Brickman, who told me to write this. Sincere thanks to Terrence McNally, John Caird, Finty Williams, Alex Timbers, Patrick Pacheco, Jack O'Brien, Barry Edelstein, Sir Patrick Stewart, and Michael Elice, whose words, along with Nancy's and Marshall's, have been reprinted here. To friends and counselors, Christian Borle, Celia Keenan-Bolger, Alan Siegel, Gordon Dickerson, Rosemary Bentinck, Kate Wetherhead, Dr. Jane Weiss and Joe Machota, for nothing less than life and work. To Tom Schumacher, whose friendship with Rog and me has been life-changing in so many ways, and who, with the prescience of all great minds, introduced me to Wendy Lefkon, the publisher and editor of this book. Via Wendy, I met Richard Curtis, whose guidance of this undertaking has been invaluable.

A loud huzzah for Winnie Ho and Al Giuliani, for this sumptuous design; Arlene Goldberg, who did the layout and composition; Joan Marcus, Tom Bloom, Jeremy Daniel, and Tom Bachtell for their generosity and their art; Jennifer Black and Warren Meislin, copy editors; Monica Vasquez, Kingswell managing editor, who kept the whole project on track; Marybeth Tregarthen, for making it look like a million bucks; and Jeanne Mosure for saying "yes."

Also, my dear parents, Roz and Harold, and brother and sister-in-law, Michael and JoAnn, who have labored hard to keep me from the dark side, the lure of which, since Rog departed, is often very strong. Let me mention, too, Dr. Henry Friedman, of the Duke University Cancer Institute, who advised us during the last weeks of Roger's life, and has, remarkably, called me every single week since.

Finally, I'd like to acknowledge Trevor Nunn, without whose recognition of Roger's raw talent way back when, we'd never have met. Trevor wrote to me recently to say how, whenever he explains how important the creation of an ensemble is, he always talks about Rog, about how it is possible for someone to be a leader and, at the same time, an equal member of the group. For finding that perfect description of Roger Rees, my thanks. And thank you, Roger, for finding me.